Core Healing

from Sexual Abuse

A Journey of Hope

Marti Wibbels, MS, LMHC

Scripture quotations marked AMP are taken from the Amplified® Bible, Copyright © 1954, 1958, 1962, 1964, 1965, 1987 by The Lockman Foundation Used by permission. (www.Lockman.org)

Scripture quotations marked ESV are taken from The Holy Bible, English Standard Version® (ESV®), copyright © 2001 by Crossway, a publishing ministry of Good News Publishers. Used by permission. All rights reserved.

Scripture quotations marked GW are taken from GOD'S WORD®, © 1995 God's Word to the Nations. Used by permission of Baker Publishing Group. All rights reserved.

Scripture quotations marked NASU are taken from the New American Standard Bible®- Update Edition, Copyright © 1960, 1962, 1963, 1968, 1971, 1972, 1973,1975, 1977, 1995 by The Lockman Foundation. Used by permission. (www.Lockman.org)

Scripture quotations marked NET are taken from the NET Bible® copyright ©1996-2006 by Biblical Studies Press, L.L.C. Used by permission. All rights reserved.

Scripture quotations marked NIV are taken from HOLY BIBLE, NEW INTERNATIONAL VERSION®. Copyright © 1973, 1978, 1984 by International Bible Society. Used by permission of Zondervan Publishing House. All rights reserved.

Scripture quotations marked NKJV are taken from the New King James Version®. Copyright © 1982 by Thomas Nelson, Inc. Used by permission. All rights reserved.

Scripture quotations marked NLT are taken from the Holy Bible, New Living Translation, copyright 1996, 2004. Used by permission of Tyndale House Publishers, Inc., Wheaton, Illinois 60189. All rights reserved.

Scripture quotations marked THE MESSAGE are taken from *THE MESSAGE*. Copyright © by Eugene H. Peterson 1993, 1994, 1995, 1996, 2000, 2001, 2002. Used by permission of NavPress Publishing Group.

For more information or to order:

Palm Beach Counseling

561.620.0089 · www.pbcounseling.com/resources

ISBN 978-0-9746124-1-6
Library of Congress Control Number: 2011909956

Printed in the United States by Morris Publishing®
3212 East Highway 30, Kearney, NE 68847
1-800-650-7888

Cover design: Doug Sykes - Cover Photograph: Alan Wibbels

Acknowledgments

This book would not have been written without the consistent work and encouragement of my beloved husband, Alan. He expertly formatted the entire book and found pull-out quotes to illustrate each concept of Core Healing. Without complaint, he reformatted chapters whenever I made major changes to the manuscript. I am grateful for his love, care and support—as well as his countless hours of exceptional work!

I appreciate the Core Healing Prayer Team who faithfully prayed throughout the writing process. Thank you to our three daughters: Kristen McHargue (who urged the formation of a prayer team in the first place!), Amy Weeks and Carrie VanTuyl and to each other member of the prayer team: Criss Bertling, Julie Brown, Jennifer Conklin, Linda Doran, Leah Feldman, Andre and Nadya Furmanov, Ivana Meservey, Don Morgan, Tim and Sherri Peterson, Suzan Sarris, Joe and Susan Sharp, Jeremy and Sarah Smith, Brenda Souto, Kimberly Stober, Kay Tira, Erin Wibbels, Gregg and Linda Wibbels and Rodger and Sarah Wittmann. Your prayers, from various parts of the world, have been answered. Thank you for investing your time to pray.

Thank you to Rosaura H. Zeghir for her work translating Core Healing into Spanish! While completing her psychology degree, she began the translation process, skillfully making it possible for Spanish-speaking people to discover new hope and healing.

The wonderful editorial work of Don Morgan and Kay Tira has been invaluable throughout this project. They spotted errors I totally missed and cared about making this book helpful for each of its readers. Thank you, Don and Kay, for sharing your time and expertise! I also appreciate excellent input from Leah Feldman and Emily Weeks during the final phase of editing.

To the hundreds of men, women, teenagers and children from dozens of countries who are applying Core Healing in their lives, I am grateful for your commitment to be healed. Your lives have forever changed my life. Seeing you triumph over tragedy helps me look forward to the victory still others can experience in their own healing journeys.

Table of Contents

Now may the God of hope fill you with all joy and peace in believing, that you may abound in hope by the power of the Holy Spirit.

Romans 15:13, NKJV

Introduction

Opening a book is like beginning an adventure. This book is designed for survivors of sexual abuse, to provide an opportunity for you to begin a healing journey that can transform your life. As with any adventure, there might be some challenges—and some surprises—included in the experience.

If you are someone who is intimately acquainted with an abuse survivor, this book can help you understand your friend or family member and perhaps even open new avenues to hope and healing in your relationship. You can join us on our healing journey. Though the comments are written mainly to abuse survivors, gaining new insights and awareness can benefit anyone.

Sexual abuse is frequently misunderstood or ignored. Survivors are often afraid to speak up—or are told not to. Yet the problem of sexual abuse is endemic throughout the world. Every time someone is silenced, the problem continues to grow; like cancer, molestation delivers unrestrained destruction when it is silently left alone.

The majority of sexual abuse victims are molested by someone they know, not by a stranger. Sexual abuse is referred to as incest when the perpetrator—the person committing sexually-offending behavior—is a family member. Extreme damage similar to that of incestual abuse occurs when sexual abuse is committed by someone whose expected behavior is to protect children and youth, such as a family friend, teacher, club leader, pastor, priest, youth worker, or camp counselor. Sexual abuse delivers incalculable harm when those in a position of trust misuse their power and influence.

Sexual abuse occurs when an adult or adolescent uses a child, young person or adult for sexual gratification without that person's informed consent. Under no circumstance can a child or adolescent give informed consent to having his or her body used sexually by another human being, though perpetrators often manipulate children or teenagers to feel as though the abusive behavior is desirable. Any form of sexual molestation delivers devastating emotional, physical, spiritual and/or intellectual damage, because human beings were not designed to be used, coerced, manipulated, deceived or dominated by other human beings.

Survivors of sexual abuse are often referred to as "numb survivors" or "people with frozen emotions," because they have so deadened their feelings that they aren't even aware how much healing needs to occur. If emotions were a child's paint box, survivors have perhaps learned to live at either the black or white end of the paint box, missing the spectrum of colors in between. If you are a survivor of abuse, you might not even realize you aren't feeling a full range of emotions. Perhaps you are one of the many survivors who have learned to deaden pain with activities, or something or someone else.

The extensive damage of sexual abuse occurs at the core of a person's being, which will be explained throughout this workbook. One complication of core damage is that it cannot be seen. If you were healing from fractured bones in both of your legs, your damage would mainly be "unseen," also. However, you would not be expected to run a race with broken legs. No one would argue that you would need time to heal, or that you would likely need long-term medical care. But the extensive damage experienced by survivors of sexual abuse, invisible to the untrained eye, is often ignored. The survivors themselves don't know what is wrong, why they feel "different," or why they can't seem to "fit in" with others. Some force themselves to keep working, feeling like they have a low-grade emotional "fever" every day. Some feel shame; others feel sad. Some feel overwhelmed; others feel hopeless, bitter, guilty or angry. Many don't feel at all.

If you want to become fully alive, the process begins with a choice to heal. That choice must be followed by consistent, intentional healing choices. Are you willing to make daily changes and take purposeful steps into all the "colors" of life? Your healing will be a unique experience, unlike anyone else's healing in some ways and like others' healing in other ways.

One reason it is difficult to persevere through the healing process is that loved ones and friends rarely understand the complexity or damage inherent in sexual abuse. If you are a family member or close friend of a survivor, it is important for you to realize he or she is not purposefully deadening emotions or ignoring the problem. It is simply too painful to allow oneself to feel without knowing *how* to move beyond the pain. If you are a survivor, you may have dismissed your own pain because you don't know how to face it and move beyond it.

Another deterrent to healing is comparing your journey to others' healing journeys. You are unique; so are they. You can make the choice to live your life, learning to make choices that will help you enjoy each moment. If you choose to avoid comparing your journey to anyone else's journey, you will free up intellectual and emotional energy to help you go forward.

Core Healing helps you understand the areas impacted by sexual abuse—and provides measurable goals for each phase of your recovery. Don't be afraid of the process; it is an opportunity for you to move forward in life. Each goal can be tailored to fit your needs and situation. Family members and friends of survivors can help *if they are asked* to come alongside in the healing process. However, the process needs to be chosen by and completed by the one who was abused. It is a private and personal healing process—and the healing journey is unique to each one completing it.

Each of the twelve chapters of this workbook has five sections; each section is designed for you to work on for about 30 minutes daily. Some chapters have a bonus section to be completed during the weekend or whenever you have time. The extra section explores the possible impact sexual abuse has during each developmental stage that can continue throughout other stages of development. It also gives ideas to help you experience restoration from developmental disruption.

The Core Five

Chapter One

To begin, it is essential to know five core areas affected by sexual abuse; each is foundational to your optimum functioning as a human being. The following acrostic provides a simple way to remember the core areas damaged by abuse:

Crime
Scene
Investigation
Plan **B**

The acrostic's first three letters, CSI, represent **Crime Scene Investigation**. Sexual abuse *is* a crime, but its survivors do not heal if they simply remain at the crime scene, inspecting—or ignoring—its horrors for the rest of their lives. Healing can begin with a choice to move beyond the crime scene into **Plan B.**

Utilizing the **CSIPB** acrostic as a mnemonic technique, consider five areas at the core of your being, which are significantly damaged in varying degrees by sexual abuse:

Competence
Security
Identity
Purpose
Belonging

Individuals who realize there has been a disruption in any of the five areas can apply *Core Healing* to learn how to move away from the crime scene into Plan B, discovering a pathway to healing and growth. Each lesson provides specific tools to help you experience freedom, change and hope.

Take a moment to consider each core concern, below. Circle the ones in which you sense a need to experience healing.

Competence   Security   Identity   Purpose   Belonging

Seven chapters in this workbook focus on the above core areas; the other five chapters address other important concerns. Each chapter has a core healing goal. The first goal is below.

Core Healing Goal: to understand the scope of sexual abuse.

ဆ ‍ య

Sexual abuse is like a bolt of lightning that strikes us at our very core. It's more than an attack on our body; it's an assault on our emotions, mind, and spirit. Part of our being is completely frozen in that moment of betrayal, confusion, sadness, hurt, and shame.[1]

Nicole Braddock
Bromley

ဆ ‍ య

1. Day One: **Defining the Challenge**

Sexual abuse is an act of power and control that takes a sexual form. A number of sources estimate that as many as one in four females and one in six males have been sexually abused by age 18. This crime occurs in secret and is often unreported, but a mere numerical estimate cannot begin to describe the catastrophic human damage caused by sexual molestation.

Sexual abuse is not about love, healthy sexuality or intimacy. The resultant damage is complex for many reasons. Often perpetrators of sexual abuse cunningly manipulate their victims, using a relationship of trust to convince another human being that the harm they propose is a "good" thing.

Molestation delivers confusion, undeserved shame and despair. Erogenous zones were designed by God to feel good. When some children are touched in a sexual way, they can't understand why something that feels pleasurable leaves them feeling horrible afterwards. For others, every second of molestation feels terrifying and repulsive. Survivors often blame themselves for what happened rather than realizing that none of the blame is theirs at all.

Savvy predators know how to deflect blame onto their prey. Some perpetrators coerce their victims, demanding they submit to molestation, using threats or intimidation to force compliance to hideous exploitation. When a child is told her mother will be killed if she doesn't let "Uncle Tommy" touch her private parts, she likely will comply and seldom will tell. When a teenage boy is told "Aunt Louise" will go to jail if he tells anyone what they do after school, he will likely remain silent.

Children learn "normal" behavior from the adults in their lives. If they are told this is what all kids do, how will they discover the truth about healthy human behavior?

Still other persons with sexually-offending behavior deceive their victims, preying on children or teenagers who are lonely, using their natural longing for companionship and relationship for their own evil purposes. They promise their victims anything while they groom them to yield their rights to their own bodies. Some say, "Nobody else loves you the way I do. I'll treat you just like my own little girl—or boy." The only part of that statement that is true is "MY OWN." Perpetrators treat victims as though they belong to *them*, as nothing more than inanimate property.

Using gifts, some shrewd sexual offenders lure their victims with uncanny skill and tenacity. "Hey, how about a trip to Disney World this weekend?" Or "I have a new phone with your name on it. Come with me for a second to my house and it's all yours." Some teenage perpetrators manipulate their victims by convincing them that "this is what the cool kids do."

ॐ ☙

Childhood sexual abuse victims quickly adapt to the abuse by implementing one of two methods to distinguish to whom they can give their trust: either they trust no one or they trust everyone.[2]

Sandra Knauer, LCSW

ॐ ☙

2

Still other predators drug their victims so they won't be able to put up any resistance at all. There are others who wait in parks, parties, hallways, or stores, looking for anyone they can catch in their secret traps.

Parents need to teach their children healthy behavior so they aren't vulnerable to manipulation, coercion, bribes or lies. But even children who have been carefully taught can succumb to the wiles of a practiced predator. Like unsuspecting fish biting on a lure, the victims don't know what is coming.

You'll notice throughout the book that I refer to you as a "survivor" of sexual abuse. It is only in this chapter that you will be referred to as a "victim," because you *were* a victim. Another human being preyed on you, using your body for selfish sexual gratification, robbing you of your dignity and eroding your self-worth. The goal of this book is to help you live not only as a person who has survived sexual abuse but as someone who *thrives* and lives the rest of your life as "more than a conqueror" (Romans 8:37).

It is vital that you understand and deal with any root issues fueled by the trauma of sexual abuse. Posttraumatic stress disorder, PTSD, is one diagnosis that pertains to some survivors of sexual trauma; the term itself indicates the trauma of sexual abuse occurred sometime in the person's **past**. As you learn about issues related to abuse, it is vital to know your life doesn't have to be defined by your past trauma. This workbook can help you move to an entirely different life, to a future of hope.

In order for you to heal, it is important to understand that numerous behaviors are considered sexual molestation. Each type of abuse can cause core damage. The following partial list includes some of the many forms of sexual abuse (note – penetration is not necessary for an incident to be considered sexual abuse). Check [✓] and underline each type of molestation you have experienced.

[ ] Fondling and/or French kissing

[ ] Exhibitionism (a stranger exposing his/her genitals)

[ ] Seductive or suggestive talk; sexual taunting or teasing

[ ] Showing a child pornography or filming a child in sexual poses

[ ] Nudity (either the perpetrator's full or partial nakedness or coercing a victim to expose any body part, especially sexual organs or breasts)

[ ] Exposing someone to others' sexual behavior

[ ] Oral sex

[ ] Anal sex; having objects forced into one's anus

[ ] Bestiality (seeing or experiencing sexual acts with animals)

[ ] Masturbation (coerced to observe and/or perform self-stimulation)

ဆ ဝ

Parents need to teach their children healthy behavior so they aren't vulnerable to manipulation, coercion, bribes or lies. But even children who have been carefully taught can succumb to the wiles of a practiced predator.

ဆ ဝ

[ ] Intercourse

[ ] Human sexual trafficking

2. Day Two: **Possible Results of Sexual Abuse**

The effects of sexual molestation vary, depending on many factors. How you are affected by abuse is influenced by your temperament as well as the severity, intensity and duration of your abuse. If you grew up in a nurturing, loving home and continue to have supportive relationships, the impact of your abuse might be less problematic than that of someone whose childhood was marked by long-term neglect and numerous forms of trauma. On the other hand, a rape could have so shattered your life that you are unable to trust even those who genuinely love and care for you.

Regardless of a person's upbringing, environment or temperament, sexual abuse wreaks havoc on human souls, minds and bodies. Its impact is so widespread that it is usually impossible to move beyond it without focused effort and help.

Below and continuing on the following two pages are over seventy of the many potential repercussions of sexual abuse. As you read the list, please note that there are other possible physical, mental or emotional factors that cause similar symptoms.

As you read the possible results of sexual abuse below, check [✓] all that apply.

❑ Nightmares—intrusive dreams with either specific trauma content or unclear, troubling content

❑ Difficulty either falling or staying asleep

❑ Either excessive interest in or avoidance of anything of a sexual nature, e.g., avoiding marital intimacy

❑ Withdrawing from others; isolating

❑ Bulimia nervosa, anorexia nervosa or binge eating disorder

❑ Refusing to participate in enjoyable activities with others

❑ Believing something is wrong with you or that you're a social misfit

❑ Feeling damaged or shameful

❑ Depression

❑ Anxiety

❑ Fearfulness

❑ Addictions, such as alcoholism, substance abuse, or sexual compulsions

❑ Behavior problems

❑ Angry outbursts

ℰℭ

Sexual abuse exacts a terrible price in the victim's life in terms of shame, contempt, and denial. The sins of the perpetrator continue to color the victim's life through an inability to enjoy relationship, intimacy, and hope. The victim's soul feels bound to denial; the heart feels wounded and alone.[3]

Dr. Dan B. Allender

ℰℭ

- ❏ Suicidal ideation
- ❏ Believing you are worthless
- ❏ Self-harm (cutting yourself, banging your head or body against a wall, or other injurious behaviors)
- ❏ Recurrent distressing recollections of the abuse
- ❏ Feeling like the trauma is recurring even when it is not
- ❏ Hypervigilance (e.g. checking throughout the night to be sure doors and windows are locked)
- ❏ Easily startled
- ❏ Difficulty concentrating
- ❏ Feeling distressed when something—like a sound, smell, taste, sight, touch, or person— triggers a memory of the abuse
- ❏ Believing you'll die young
- ❏ Believing you can never enjoy life
- ❏ Self-criticism or self-doubt
- ❏ Inability to trust in people
- ❏ Inappropriate behavior
- ❏ Insecurity
- ❏ Aggressiveness
- ❏ Codependent behavior
- ❏ Do not like being touched and/or hugged
- ❏ Learning problems
- ❏ Abuse replication
- ❏ Guilt
- ❏ Inferiority
- ❏ Trying to be "perfect"
- ❏ Chaotic existence
- ❏ Disillusionment or a sense of futility
- ❏ Loss of hope
- ❏ Overemphasis on peers
- ❏ Risky behavior
- ❏ Too much focus on outward appearance
- ❏ Fear of emotional, intellectual, physical or spiritual intimacy
- ❏ Inability to trust in God
- ❏ Loss of purpose
- ❏ Derealization—feeling detached from reality or one's surroundings

ℰℭ

Sexual abuse doesn't devastate only a victim's internal world. Whatever damage is done internally will eventually affect the external, observable life.[4]

Dr. Dan B. Allender

ℰℭ

- ❑ Bitterness
- ❑ Cynicism
- ❑ Dissociating—sometimes feeling separate from your body, especially during a memory of the abuse
- ❑ Physiological reactions when reminded of the molestation
- ❑ Poor body image
- ❑ Terror about having a doctor physically examine you
- ❑ Feeling powerless and afraid when having a dental examination, especially when the dentist or hygienist leans over you
- ❑ Feeling sexual when afraid, lonely, sad, used, degraded, hurt or mad
- ❑ Not being able to recognize when people are using you
- ❑ Trying to be friends with people who don't care
- ❑ Inability to recall important details of past abuse
- ❑ Remaining loyal to people who continually betray you
- ❑ Repeating similar painful experiences over and over
- ❑ Being attracted to people who are not trustworthy or not knowing who is safe
- ❑ Not noticing physical or emotional pain
- ❑ Keeping secrets for someone who molested you
- ❑ Spending more time in fantasy than in reality
- ❑ Destructive sexual desires
- ❑ Despair
- ❑ Believing you will always be a victim
- ❑ Feeling like you need to rescue others
- ❑ Feeling like others want to persecute you
- ❑ Experiencing confusion about life
- ❑ Physical pain and/or health concerns

Each of the potential consequences of sexual abuse could be a study in itself. In fact, there are books that deal with many ramifications of abuse, such as anger, depression, self-harm, addictive behaviors, codependency or PTSD. This study focuses on core areas, because as those heal, you can experience significant change and growth in other areas of life as well.

At various times in the workbook, suggestions will be given for finding additional help or reading a specific book, if indicated. Since other emotional, mental and physiological conditions can be comorbid—occurring simultaneously with ramifications of sexual abuse—be sure you obtain appropriate professional help if you are experiencing concerns such as

As we get older and learn about other people's lives, we eventually learn that not everyone lived in a world just like ours.[5]

Nicole Braddock Bromley

suicidal ideation, debilitating depression or anxiety, eating disorders, addictive behaviors, etc.

3. Day Three: **Why Core Healing?**

The damage of sexual abuse occurs in the core of your being—in your sense of competence, security, identity, purpose and belonging—and that is where healing needs to occur. For each of those areas to heal, the real healing needs to begin in your mind. As the poet John Milton said, "The mind is its own place, and it itself can make a Heaven of Hell, a Hell of Heaven." Core Healing can help your hellish experiences be transformed by a new way of thinking, feeling and living.

You do not have to stay in the state of trauma caused by your sexual abuse. Every day of your work in *Core Healing* is designed to help you move beyond the abuse, growing into a new way of living and enjoying life! As you experience healing, the ramifications of abuse will no longer define you.

Imagine someone going to the doctor because of extreme exhaustion, stating, "I am so tired I can't even go to work." The physician wouldn't simply say, "Try to get eight hours of sleep each night." No, a good physician would carefully consider the patient's diverse symptoms; obtain blood samples; and complete other appropriate medical tests or referrals. If test results indicated that the patient had cancer, the physician would treat the cancer, not the exhaustion. The exhaustion was a *symptom* of a potentially fatal illness, not the illness itself. Similarly, each ramification of sexual molestation is symptomatic of a larger concern that must be addressed.

As you consider the symptoms of sexual abuse you have experienced, notice which of the core areas seems affected by each. In the spaces below or on a separate page, note any of Day Two's Results of Sexual Abuse—or others not mentioned on the list—that seem to apply in any of the five core areas (there are no right or wrong answers; just thinking about this will increase your awareness and help you on your healing journey).

Competence: _____
_____
_____
_____

Security: _____
_____
_____
_____
_____

ဆ ၷ

Sexual abuse does not have to define you for the rest of your life. Core Healing can help you move away from the trauma of the past into a future of hope.

ဆ ၷ

Identity: _____

_____

_____

_____

Purpose: _____

_____

_____

_____

Belonging: _____

_____

_____

_____

4. Day Four: **A New Perspective**

While sexual abuse is motivated by someone's evil desire to selfishly control and use another human being, God has an entirely different motivation. His desire is to bring you profound healing and hope. Right now, that might be difficult to comprehend, particularly since sexual molestation often robs people of their ability to trust anyone—especially God.

For a few moments, please set aside your hurt or preconceptions to consider another perspective.

 Explore - Jesus said, *Whoever receives one little child like this in My name receives Me. Whoever causes one of these little ones who believe in Me to sin, it would be better for him if a millstone were hung around his neck, and he were drowned in the depth of the sea.*

Matthew 18:5-6, NKJV

You didn't sin when you were sexually abused. The sin was entirely that of the person or persons who molested you. And Jesus hates what happened to you!

Can you imagine Him telling your abuser "it would be better for [you] if a millstone were hung around [your] neck, and [you] were drowned in the depth of the sea"? ____ Yes ____ No Journal how you are feeling as you think about Jesus' statement. _____

_____

_____

_____

_____

As you turn your attention to Me [Jesus], feel the Light of My Presence shining upon you. Open your mind and heart to receive My heavenly smile of approval Let My gold-tinged Love wash over you and soak into the depths of your being.[6]

Sarah Young

Describe how it feels to consider that God never wanted your abuse to happen, that it was entirely the choice of the one who committed the criminal behavior against you. _____

_____

_____

_____

_____

_____

God talks about the poor spiritual choices of people who hurt others.

 Explore - *You worship your idols with great passion beneath the oaks and under every green tree. You sacrifice your children down in the valleys, among the jagged rocks in the cliffs. Your gods are the smooth stones in the valleys. You worship them with liquid offerings and grain offerings. They, not I, are your inheritance. Do you think all this makes me happy?*

Isaiah 57:5-6, NLT

In a real sense, wounding someone through sexual molestation is a form of idolatry, of people worshipping their own evil desires rather than God.

For from within, out of men's hearts, come evil thoughts, sexual immorality, theft, murder, adultery, greed, malice, deceit, lewdness, envy, slander, arrogance and folly. Mark 7:21-22, NIV

It does not please God to see His beloved creation suffering at the hands of people who willfully rebel against Him. The touches of sexual abuse hurt, but God's touch is tender and compassionate. When He says we are to come to Him like children, it is because children are born with an amazing ability to trust others; to believe in God. When sexual abuse occurs, the resultant loss of hope, joy and trust is a travesty not only against their bodies but their souls.

Imagine for a moment that God wants you to experience hope like you've never experienced; joy like you can't imagine—and peace for the rest of your life. Write about what that might look like for you: _____

_____

_____

_____

_____

_____

_____

> ❧ ❦
>
> When we find the courage to tell, we take the first major step on our healing journey. When we embrace the truth that the abuse wasn't our fault, we take the second. But there are other lies that can cause us more problems and pain along the way. Chief among them are the lies we believe about God. Replacing these lies with the truth is crucial for healing; for what we believe about God is the source of everything we believe about ourselves, others, and the world.[7]
>
> Nichole Braddock Bromley
>
> ❧ ❦

If a miracle happened tonight and you awoke with a life free from the debilitating ramifications of the trauma of sexual abuse, what changes might you experience tomorrow? _____

_____

_____

_____

_____

5. Day Five: **Psychosocial Development**

In some future chapters, psychosocial development will be addressed as "weekend bonus work." For this chapter, it is included as Day Five, simply because this chapter already contains so much information that you may need the weekend to review what we've already covered.

The age(s) at which your sexual abuse occurred could have disrupted your overall development. In psychology, psychosocial theory considers the complex interactions among biological, psychological and societal systems throughout a person's lifespan. As you consider each stage of your psychosocial development, you can discover new ways to grow. Even if a chapter isn't addressing the age at which your molestation occurred, it can be helpful to be aware of typical developmental progress.

 The first stage of psychosocial development, infancy, is from birth to age two. At this stage, development occurs when a baby experiences what is referred to as "mutuality" with his or her caregiver. That means when he or she cries, someone responds with nurturing care. Hope, optimism and trust develop when a baby realizes someone is available to provide for felt needs. [8]

_____

_____

_____

_____

Did anyone respond to your cries? Babies are often mute in orphanages where no one responds, rocking back and forth in their cribs without making a sound. Did you learn to not to cry, not to ask for what you need? Explain. _____

_____

_____

_____

_____

Therefore if any person is [ingrafted] in Christ (the Messiah) he is a new creation (a new creature altogether); the old [previous moral and spiritual condition] has passed away. Behold, the fresh and new has come!

2 Corinthians 5:17, AMP

If you did not experience mutuality with your caregiver at this first stage of development, you probably have difficulty trusting anyone. You also might find it difficult to form lasting relationships. Do you withdraw from others or do you feel safe in relationships? Journal your experience below.

_____

_____

_____

_____

_____

_____

_____

_____

_____

If you experienced sexual abuse at this stage of development, you likely have no memory of the abuse, because we require language to have verbal memories. You might have been told about molestation that occurred at this stage, or you might have a vague unrest about people who were in your life during infancy. Write down your thoughts here. _____

_____

_____

_____

_____

_____

_____

_____

Paste a baby picture of yourself* in the space on the right, and imagine your adult self is talking with your baby self. If you experienced disrupted development at this stage, you can "reframe" this stage of development by writing down several specific ways you could have experienced positive care from birth to age two.

* If you don't have a baby picture, you can paste a picture from a magazine here, or you can draw a picture of yourself as a baby.

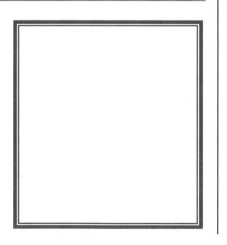

     80   03

All of us recognize that there is no such thing as a perfect parent. All of us are descended from imperfect parents, and grew up in imperfect families. But to acknowledge this as an intellectual proposition is one thing. To actually admit that our parents have failed us is for some of us, a very hard thing to do.[9]

Dr. David Stoop
Dr. James Masteller

80   03

Think about the first stage of psychosocial development. Imagine yourself being brought to Jesus, as described in Luke 18:15 (NIV) *"People were also bringing babies to Jesus to have him touch them."* Let Jesus touch your pain and give you new hope. He cares. He comforts! What would Jesus say to you as you come to Him? _____

_____

_____

_____

_____

_____

_____

_____

_____

_____

_____

_____

_____

_____

_____

_____

_____

_____

_____

Write a prayer, asking Him to help you as continue your healing journey.

_____

_____

_____

_____

_____

_____

_____

_____

_____

_____

_____

I [Jesus] am perpetually with you, taking care of you. That is the most important fact of your existence. I am not limited by time or space; My Presence with you is a forever-promise. You need not fear the future, for I am already there.[10]

Sarah Young

Five Growth Areas

Chapter Two

Last week, you considered the impact of sexual abuse on five areas at the core of your being. This week, we are going to look at five essential areas of growth—emotional, intellectual, physical, spiritual and social. Though each of these areas can be significantly damaged by sexual abuse, you can experience profound healing in all of these vital aspects of life.

Core Healing Goal: to recognize potential for growth and choices you can make in five distinct areas of your life.

1. Day One: **Emotional Growth**

   Pause and observe the emotions or feelings you're experiencing today. After reading the list of emotions below, circle the ones you're sensing:

Excitement	Sadness	Numb	Happiness
Hope	Anger	Hurt	Irritation
Frustration	Depression	Disappointment	Fear
Bitterness	Anxiety	Offended	Grief

   Other emotions, moods or feelings I'm experiencing that are not listed include _____

   _____

   _____

   Review the items you circled or listed. Check how often you experience them in the appropriate column below.

Emotion/Mood/Feeling	Daily	Weekly	Often

ഏ ൙

This is where the healing starts

When you come to where you're broken within

The light meets the dark[11]

Tenth Avenue North
Healing Begins (Lyrics)

ഏ ൙

13

Please read Henri Nouwen's statement, and describe any ways you relate to it: "A little criticism makes me angry, and a little rejection makes me depressed. A little praise raises my spirits, and a little success excites me. It takes very little to raise me up or thrust me down. Often I am like a small boat on the ocean, completely at the mercy of its waves. All the time and energy I spend in keeping some kind of balance and preventing myself from being tipped over and drowning shows my life is mostly a struggle for survival; not a holy struggle, but an anxious struggle resulting from the mistaken idea that it is the world that defines me."[12]

I relate to Henri Nouwen when I am _____

_____

_____

_____

_____

_____

_____

2. Day Two: **Intellectual Growth**

What have you been thinking about today? _____

_____

_____

_____

_____

_____

_____

_____

_____

_____

Think about the connection between your thoughts and your feelings. Describe how *what* you have been thinking about could have influenced how you feel today. _____

_____

_____

_____

_____

_____

_____

_____

_____

ஐ ෆ

Feelings must be engaged. They are meant to be involved. [Yet] our danger is to submit ourselves to our feelings and to allow them to dictate to us, to govern and to master us and to control the whole of our lives.[13]

Martyn Lloyd-Jones

ஐ ෆ

14

Nouwen describes experiencing "*an anxious struggle resulting from the mistaken idea that it is the world that defines me.*" Are there any ways in which either your past abuse or present situation is defining you?

_____

_____

_____

_____

_____

_____

_____

_____

_____

3. Day Three: **Physical Growth**

Write down the age you are today: _____

Write down the age(s) you were when you were sexually abused. _____

_____

Are there any ways your physical growth was affected by sexual abuse? If your answer is "yes," write down specific effects you have observed or wondered about regarding your physical development: _____

_____

_____

_____

_____

_____

_____

_____

Write a sentence or two describing how you would like to be able to look at your body now: _____

_____

_____

_____

_____

_____

_____

80 CB

The Lord is my shepherd; I have all that I need. He lets me rest in green meadows; he leads me beside peaceful streams. He renews my strength. He guides me along right paths, bringing honor to his name. Even when I walk through the darkest valley, I will not be afraid, for you are close beside me.

Psalm 23:1-4, NLT

80 CB

People who sexually abuse others want to gain power and look for someone vulnerable to their coercion. They take control of the defenseless. At its core, sexual abuse is an act of power and control. Do you still feel powerless? Why or why not? _____

_____

_____

_____

_____

Many survivors of sexual abuse ask, "If God is all-powerful and all loving, why does He permit evil and suffering in the world?" Throughout history, people have tried to answer this question, but many times the answers raise more questions than solutions.

God created an unblemished world where there was no disease, no cruelty, and no crime. God's creation was perfect. When He finished His creation on the seventh day, *"God saw all that he had made, and it was very good"* (Genesis 1:31, NIV).

God gave Adam and Eve dominion over the world. They were two perfect people living in a perfect environment, and yet they chose to rebel against God. When they rebelled, they set in motion a series of events that changed the nature of man and the nature of creation. Both were affected by sin. Instead of being a perfect paradise, creation itself began deteriorating. People became sinful and hated God. The more they rejected God, the more they experienced the consequences of their actions. Evil spread throughout creation, bringing with it disease, destruction and entropy to a world that had been unblemished. And, people began to choose to hurt each other in ways that previously were unthinkable.

Many people blame God for not stopping their molestation and wonder, "Why didn't He make the abuse stop?"

Have you ever felt like that? ____ Yes ____ No If you answered "yes," take a moment to wonder what the world would be like if people allowed God to help them treat each other with love and kindness, and live as He says to live. Write your thoughts below.

_____

_____

_____

_____

_____

_____

ജ ഗ

The very fact that faith looks to a power beyond itself means that it is continually subject to loss of control. So if you're looking to get control of all your problems, forget Christianity. If you're looking for success, happiness, or freedom from pain, forget Christ. The way of Christ is the cross, and the cross spells weakness, poverty, failure, death.[14]

Mike Mason

ജ ഗ

Can people at the same time have freedom and be forced by God to do the right thing? ___ Yes ___ No Explain. _____

_____

_____

_____

_____

_____

_____

_____

Life—Embezzled!

A person being brought to trial for embezzling has stolen something from someone else, often an employer who previously viewed the person as trustworthy. Merriam-Webster's explains that the word "embezzle" comes from the Anglo-French *embesiller*, which means "to make away with," from *en-* + *besiller*, which means "to steal, plunder." Seldom would anyone blame God for the robbery of embezzlement because of clear awareness that the person, the embezzler, willfully chose to rob another human being or organization.

An embezzler is a person who takes something for one's own use in violation of a trust. A sexual abuser is a person who violates a trust—that of caring for other people, treating them with dignity and respect. And the molester also takes that person for his or her own selfish indulgence. Remember, sexual abuse is an act of power that takes a sexual form.

Imagine that the person(s) who abused you is another type of "embezzler," fully responsible for his or her own choices. Though you cannot regain the stage of development that was robbed from you, you can recover the growth God designed to occur in your life at that time. You can release yourself from the past trauma and make your own choice to go forward, trusting God rather than blaming Him. He did not choose you to be abused; He did choose you to be healed and whole.

Colossians 3:21 (NASU) says, *"Fathers, do not exasperate your children, so that they will not lose heart."* If you have lost heart, you can allow God to restore your heart—and your hope.

Every person has a choice—to have good or bad behavior, to do the right thing or wrong things, to treat people with dignity and respect or to treat people horribly, even abusively. Regardless of what *people* have done to your body, you can reclaim it now and begin to live in new ways. The apostle Paul describes a new way for believers to experience physical vitality in Galatians 2:20.

ॐ ☙

I discovered that sorrow was not to be feared but rather endured with hope and expectancy that God would use it to bless my life.[15]

Jill Briscoe

ॐ ☙

Explore - *My old self has been crucified with Christ. It is no longer I who live, but Christ lives in me. So I live in this earthly body by trusting in the Son of God, who loved me and gave himself for me.*

Galatians 2:20, NLT

According to this verse, what happened to a Christian's old self? _____

_____

Have you asked Christ to live in you? _____

If so, will you allow Him to give you strength to live your life? _____

What did the Son of God do for you? _____

_____

_____

_____

_____

Explore - *The Lord also will be a refuge and a high tower for the oppressed, a refuge and a stronghold in times of trouble (high cost, destitution, and desperation). And they who know Your name [who have experience and acquaintance with Your mercy] will lean on and confidently put their trust in You, for You, Lord, have not forsaken those who seek (inquire of and for) You [on the authority of God's Word and the right of their necessity].* Psalm 9:9-10, AMP

When a person, event, or habit feels like it is overpowering you, you can claim God's provision of refuge as described in this passage. How would your life change if you accept God's gift of refuge? _____

_____

_____

_____

_____

_____

_____

4. Day Four: **Spiritual Growth**

God cherishes each person, but the child or adult who was sexually molested often doesn't feel like s/he is cherished by anyone—especially God. At this point in your journey, it can be helpful to begin looking at God as your personal Shepherd, as the one who wants to lead you, help you—and sometimes even carry you—through your healing process.

> **80 03**
>
> If you completely give of yourself physically, you become exhausted. But when you give of yourself spiritually, you get more strength. God never gives us strength for tomorrow, or for the next hour, but only for the strain of the moment.[16]
>
> Oswald Chambers
>
> **80 03**

As you read the following verses, imagine God as <u>your</u> shepherd.

 Explore - *I am the Door; anyone who enters in through Me will be saved (will live). He will come in and he will go out [freely], and will find pasture. The thief comes only in order to steal and kill and destroy. I came that they may have and enjoy life, and have it in abundance (to the full, till it overflows). I am the Good Shepherd. The Good Shepherd risks and lays down His [own] life for the sheep.* John 10:9-11, AMP

Jesus describes Himself as the door to an intimate and personal relationship with Him. Have you asked Him to come into your life? _____

If so, describe how you asked Jesus into your life and when. _____
_____
_____
_____
_____
_____
_____

If not, would you like to invite Him into your life now? _____

When Christ comes into your life, you become a child of God and Jesus became your good Shepherd. What do verses 9, 10b, and 11 say about what He wants to do for you? _____
_____
_____
_____
_____
_____
_____
_____

Jesus said He came to give you an abundant life. What do you think He meant by that? _____
_____
_____
_____
_____
_____

           ℬ   Ϫ

Shepherd of Love, You knew I had lost my way; Shepherd of Love, You cared that I'd gone astray.
You sought and found me, placed around me Strong arms that carried me home;
No foe can harm me or alarm me, never again will I roam![17]

John W. Peterson
Shepherd of Love
(Lyrics)

           ℬ   Ϫ

Who is the thief in verse 10? _____ The goal of the thief is to

_____

One of the ways Satan steals, kills, and destroys is by robbing children's innocence through sexual abuse. The sad reality is that children, adolescents and adults throughout the world are being sexually abused every day and night. This abuse is often perpetrated by someone who should be trustworthy, such as a family member, child care provider, club sponsor, teacher, older friend, neighbor, spiritual leader, etc. That molestation makes it difficult to trust anyone—even God!

Trust can only be rebuilt when you are confident that there is someone safe to trust. If you have been wounded by molestation, it is difficult to imagine ever being safe enough to allow yourself to relax and trust. You might even believe God doesn't care about you or that He wasn't there when you were being hurt.

Imagine for a moment that God wept when you were molested, that the person(s) who hurt you made hideous choices utterly outside of God's plan for you. There may have been other people who hurt you by not noticing what happened to you, by not hearing your cries for help.

Now, read Mark 10:13-16, and imagine Jesus touching **you**, grieving with you and taking your sorrows on Himself.

 Explore - *Then they brought little children to Him, that He might touch them; but the disciples rebuked those who brought them. But when Jesus saw it, He was greatly displeased and said to them, "Let the little children come to Me, and do not forbid them; for of such is the kingdom of God. Assuredly, I say to you, whoever does not receive the kingdom of God as a little child will by no means enter it." And He took them up in His arms, laid His hands on them, and blessed them.* Mark 10:13-16, NKJV

Who tried to keep the little children away from Jesus? _____

Jesus rebuked them and asked that the children be brought to Him. He touched them.

Describe what could change in your life if you trust God to touch you, to guide you into His love and healing: _____

_____

_____

_____

_____

_____

℠ ℞

Jesus said to his disciples: "Things that cause people to sin are bound to come, but woe to that person through whom they come. It would be better for him to be thrown into the sea with a millstone tied around his neck than for him to cause one of these little ones to sin.

Luke 17:1-2, NIV

℠ ℞

If it is difficult to trust God, describe your understanding of why that is so:

_____

_____

_____

_____

_____

_____

_____

Imagine Jesus looking at you; His tender eyes focused on you. He touches you, and you can see tears spilling down His cheeks. He knows your sadness; He feels your pain. He loves you and grieves that you were hurt. Will you let Him touch you and heal you? _____

 Explore - *Cast all your anxiety* [worries; cares] *on him because he cares for you.* 1 Peter 5:7, NIV

Here, Peter is referring to Christ's classic words of encouragement in the Sermon on the Mount (Matthew 6:25-32), while quoting Psalm 55:22: *"Cast your cares on the Lord and He will sustain you."* A Christian's confidence rests in the fact that Christ is genuinely concerned for your welfare.

You can give Jesus your fears and worries. He is strong enough to help you with your hurts and loving enough to give you even the faith you need to begin to trust Him. Where are you in your spiritual journey right now?

_____

_____

_____

_____

_____

_____

_____

_____

_____

_____

_____

_____

_____

_____

"There is an Indian proverb or axiom that says everyone is a house with four rooms, a physical, a mental, an emotional, and a spiritual. Most of us tend to live in one room most of the time but, unless we go into every room every day, even if only to keep it aired, we are not a complete person."[19]

Rumer Godden
A House with Four Rooms

Think about the emotional, intellectual, physical, and spiritual aspects of your life. In which area(s) do you believe you need to grow? _____

_____

_____

_____

_____

_____

Write down at least one growth goal for each area you listed.

Physical Growth Goal: _____

_____

_____

_____

Intellectual/Mental Growth Goal: _____

_____

_____

_____

Emotional Growth Goal: _____

_____

_____

_____

_____

Spiritual Growth Goal: _____

_____

_____

_____

_____

 භ ශ

The process of setting goals helps you choose where you want to go in life. By knowing precisely what you want to achieve, you know where you have to concentrate your efforts. [20]

Unknown

 භ ශ

5. Day Five: **Social Growth**

Often we treat people in our present life in ways mirroring how we were treated in childhood, unconsciously seeking a relationship that feels "normal." Unfortunately, "normal" is often defined by memories stored in our subconscious that really are not useful for our lives today.

For example, Cameron never feels comfortable in social settings. He makes sarcastic remarks about everyone and everything. When a friend seems hurt by a barb thrown her way, Cameron laughs and says, "Don't be so serious; you know I was just kidding." He seems to have no awareness of how his comments come across to others. He has repressed the painful memories of his childhood, when he was the family scapegoat, blamed for every small and large problem in his family system. Molested by older boys on the way to school as a second grader, he has never told anyone what happened to him. Now, he uses sarcasm to express the hurt stored so deeply inside him that he has forgotten it is there.

Becky hates to have anyone touch her. If a friend impulsively reaches toward Becky to hug her, she backs away, her body rigid. Volunteering together on a community project, a friend asked her, "Becky, why are you so unapproachable?" Becky responded angrily, "What are you talking about?" She felt stung by what she perceived as her friend's heartless criticism. Becky has repressed memories of sexual abuse for so long that her stored pain keeps her from enjoying even a friend's safe touch.

Think about social situations you seem to experience over and over—emotional traumas that keep repeating themselves. How might you be unconsciously re-creating the trauma of your past? _____

_____

_____

_____

_____

_____

Criticism is a mechanism many use to protect themselves from being hurt. Reflect back over the past few days. Have you surrounded yourself with the barbed wire of criticism? Can you think of times you have kept people away from you by either criticizing them—or yourself? _____

_____

_____

_____

_____

_____

৪০ ৫৪

I have told you these things, so that in me you may have peace. In this world you will have trouble. But take heart! I have overcome the world.

Jesus
John 16:33, NIV

৪০ ৫৪

If you felt abandoned in your past, are you re-creating similar emotions of abandonment in current social situations? _____

_____

_____

_____

Are you willing to look at your current concerns in a new way? _____

_____

_____

_____

Will you allow God to create a new pattern for facing social situations that doesn't repeat old patterns of abandonment, abuse or hurt?

_____ Yes _____ No Explain _____

_____

_____

_____

_____

_____

Children are the living messages we send to a time we will not see.[22]

Neil Postman

Week Two - Weekend Bonus Work

The second stage of psychosocial development is Toddlerhood, which includes ages two and three. At this stage, development occurs through the central process of imitation, which implies access to relationships and healthy communication.[21]

What was happening in your life at ages two and three? (If you aren't aware of your life at this stage of development, you could contact *safe* relatives who might be able to help you answer this question.) _____

_____

_____

_____

_____

_____

_____

_____

_____

_____

_____

_____

What relationships were important to you when you were a toddler? Who nurtured you? (If your answer is "no one," describe what you would have liked to have experienced.) _____

_____

_____

_____

_____

_____

A child learns self-control during this stage of development. Toddlers can learn to self-soothe when disappointed, while developing language and independent play skills. If you experienced sexual abuse during your toddler years, you might still be experiencing difficulty with self control. In the space below, describe any areas where this is a concern (e.g. current compulsions, shame-based behaviors, etc.). _____

_____

_____

_____

_____

_____

_____

_____

_____

_____

_____

_____

_____

 Explore - *But Jesus called the children to him and said, "Let the little children come to me, and do not hinder them, for the kingdom of God belongs to such as these. I tell you the truth, anyone who will not receive the kingdom of God like a little child will never enter it.* Luke 18:16-17, NIV

Now, picture yourself as one of the children who was actually with Jesus as He spoke. Imagine Him looking at you as a toddler. He is smiling, reaching out His arms to you. You can run into His arms and let Him comfort you. Will you? _____

_____

_____

_____

_____

_____

What would change in your life now if you choose to accept Jesus' help? _____

_____
_____
_____
_____
_____
_____
_____
_____
_____
_____

Describe what your life could be like if you were to allow Jesus to comfort you in your sorrows._____

_____
_____
_____
_____
_____
_____
_____
_____
_____
_____
_____
_____
_____
_____
_____

ᛞ ᛢ

I have set the Lord always before me; Because He is at my right hand I shall not be moved.

Psalm 16:8, NKJV

ᛞ ᛢ

"Live first and foremost in My Presence. Gradually you will become more aware of Me than of people and places around you. This awareness will not detract from your relationships with others. Instead, it will increase your ability to give love and encouragement to them. My Peace will permeate your words and demeanor. You will be active in the world, yet one step removed from it. you will not be easily shaken, because My enveloping Presence buffers the blow of problems."[23]

from "Jesus Calling" by Sarah Young (September 24)

Don't Believe Everything You Think

Chapter Three

Each of us has automatic thoughts that occur so often and so repeatedly that we usually don't even question their legitimacy. You have had years of practice—reviewing, repeating and believing what you think. As you begin to notice what you are thinking, observe how your thoughts influence your moods. Then you can train yourself to make ongoing conscious choices to identify and replace thoughts that are not helping you heal, change or grow.

Core Healing Goal: to identify and replace distorted thoughts.

1. Day One: **Identifying Recurring Thoughts**

   Below, list some of your everyday recurring thoughts. Stop and notice, then describe your resultant mood.

Common/Recurring Thought	Resultant Mood

It's essential to pay attention to your thoughts because how you **think** influences how you **feel** and what you **do**. When you realize you **don't have to believe everything you think**, you have an amazing opportunity to bring change to every area of your life. One verse that explains this process is: *"What he thinks is what he really is"* (Proverbs 23:7b, TEV). In other words, where your mind goes, your behavior usually follows.

Select one of your common thoughts (above) and describe how the resulting mood influences how you behave. _____

_____

_____

> ℅ ℃
>
> The world we have created is a product of our thinking; it cannot be changed without changing our thinking.[24]
>
> Albert Einstein
>
> ℅ ℃

2. Day Two: **Changing the Way You Think**

Changing the way you think is as difficult as learning a new language when you're an adult. But if you move to another country where a language different from your primary language is spoken, learning that country's language is essential to effectively live and communicate with the people there.

Though it's challenging to learn a new language, you know you've mastered it when you start to dream in it. With repetition, study and daily practice of words, phrases and sentences, many accomplish the goal of mastering new languages. Similarly, learning a new emotional language requires persistent choices. Conscientiously making those moment-by-moment choices can transform your healing journey.

Think about what is happening in your life now and how you have been thinking about it. In the space below, describe any thoughts (regarding concerns, fears, hurt, betrayal, worries, joy, hope, sadness, etc.) you have been focusing on repeatedly: _____

_____

_____

_____

_____

_____

_____

_____

_____

_____

_____

_____

_____

_____

_____

_____

_____

_____

_____

Today can be different from any other day. You have an opportunity to learn a new emotional language, one that accurately communicates God's love to your mind, emotions and body. As an act of your will, you can

Language is the blood of the soul into which thoughts run and out of which they grow.[25]

Oliver Wendell Holmes

28

choose to live differently and think intentionally. You can even begin to trust God to work in and through you.

 Explore - *Therefore, I urge you, brothers, in view of God's mercy, to offer your bodies as living sacrifices, holy and pleasing to God — this is your spiritual act of worship. Do not conform any longer to the pattern of this world, but be transformed by the renewing of your mind. Then you will be able to test and approve what God's will is—his good, pleasing and perfect will.*

Romans 12:1-2, NIV

3. Day Three: **Automatic Thoughts**

Automatic thoughts often occur in distorted patterns. That distorted thinking is to your mind like being in a house of mirrors is to how you see your physical body. If you've looked at your reflection in a carnival's house of mirrors, you realize you aren't ten feet tall—or ten feet wide, even if a mirror makes you seem to look that way. You know each of the mirrors presents a distorted reflection, so you choose not to accept the image of reality presented to you there.

However, a child who grew up in a house of mirrors might think she looks like the distorted reflections she has seen over and over again. And, if you have thought in distortions for weeks, months, or years, you will first need to recognize that a thought is distorted before you can make an intentional choice to change it.

The following list presents ten common types of distorted thinking, or cognitive distortions. (Both Aaron T. Beck, M.D., and David Burns, M.D., have completed extensive research regarding the impact of distorted thinking on feelings and actions. The list of cognitive distortions, below, has been influenced by their work.) **Place a check next to any of the cognitive distortions you have experienced. Place two checks if you are <u>currently</u> experiencing that type of distorted thinking.**

_____ **Emotional Reasoning:** taking your emotions as valid indicators of reality. Examples: If you feel hopeless, you see your situation as hopeless, impossible, discouraging or debilitating. If you feel sad, you become dejected, believing your life is (and always will be) miserable and/or depressing.

_____ **Jumping to Conclusions:** reacting to what you think or assume happened, was said or meant by another person without getting all of the facts. Example: When someone says "I can't go with you Saturday because I have plans," you assume, "She is saying that because I'm so [unhealthy, boring, worthless, etc.] that no one wants to be with me."

_____ **All or Nothing Thinking:** views life in black or white, good or bad. The person with this mindset is often a perfectionist, believing he or she (or someone else) is a failure if anything goes wrong in any situation, conversation, job, relationship, etc. Realizing that everyone experiences—and can survive—significant loss, disappointment, sorrows, and hurt does not occur to this mindset.

_____ **Should Thinking:** having unspoken rules about what you or others should do or should have done. Examples: "I should have known better." "He should apologize." "I am going to stay angry until she does what she should do."

_____ **Overgeneralization:** seeing one event as a never-ending pattern. For example: after failing a history exam, saying "I should just drop out of school. I am never going to make it." [The previous example combines two types of distorted thinking. In addition to Overgeneralizing, it adds Should Thinking.]

_____ **Catastrophizing:** expecting that any situation will result in disaster and believing that you are somehow destined to suffer continued hardships, misfortunes, pain and trouble. [Instead, when someone is in the midst of severe pain or challenging life circumstances, he could look at it as an opportunity to learn and grow rather than a never-ending pattern of defeat.]

_____ **Filtering:** focusing on a negative detail in any situation and dwelling on that while "filtering out" any positive aspects of the circumstance, event, person or concern. Filtering occurs any time your perspective about yourself or anyone else is limited to the negative. Even in a genuinely negative current event, you could focus on something positive you can gain instead. For example: "That group seems to be cliquish, so I'll find another group where I can make friends" avoids the negative filter that says, "I never fit in anywhere. No one wants me around, so I'll just become a loner."

_____ **Blaming & Labeling:** when you blame yourself for something beyond your control or hold others responsible for how you feel. Example: "If my parents hadn't treated me the way they did, I wouldn't feel discouraged now." "Because _____ molested me, I am a failure."

_____ **Control Myth:** either thinking you are responsible for the happiness and well-being of everyone in your life—or thinking they are somehow responsible for your well-being, since you are helpless to stop your pain [sorrow, difficulty, etc.].

_____ **Overlooking the Positive:** rejecting positive life experiences and believing they somehow don't begin to reduce the negatives you have faced, will face, or are facing now.

ഔ ര

Don't be so hard on yourself. I [Jesus] can bring good even out of your mistakes. My infinite creativity can weave both good choices and bad into a lovely design.[26]

Sarah Young

ഔ ര

30

It is vital to realize when automatic negative thoughts occur. Since you've had years of thinking the way you think today, it will take repeated, conscientious effort to reduce the occurrence of distorted thinking. Like old-style radios, your mind can emit "static" that won't fade out unless it's fine-tuned. The first step to reducing mental "static" is recognizing when your thoughts are distorted. **[For help discovering a new way of thinking, please turn to Appendix A for a list of Bible verses that can provide new perspectives to replace each type of distorted thinking.]**

Thoughts are your perception of what is happening or has happened to you. Many of the emotions you experience are generated by your thoughts. If you are experiencing genuinely difficult emotions, change can begin by being alert to the presence of distorted thinking. If you notice cognitive distortions, now is a good time to begin changing your thoughts.

Following are summaries of three stories you probably have heard before. Each of them represents distorted thinking. As you read, see if you can determine the type of distorted thinking represented (review the list on the previous two pages for ideas).

Chicken Little is a story told in various forms, one which features a chicken who believes the sky is falling when an acorn falls on her head. Fearful of impending disaster, Chicken Little warns other animals, all who eventually become dinner for a sly fox. The story seems absurd—unless you've ever been in a forest and heard the result of the wind shaking hundreds of acorns loose. As the acorns tumble to the ground, they sound like a severe hailstorm.

Look at the list of distorted thought patterns and write down any that represent Chicken Little's thought process. Describe how they could shape her fear.

_____
_____
_____
_____
_____
_____
_____
_____
_____

> ℬ ℭ
>
> Fairy Tales are more than true; not because they tell us that dragons exist, but because they tell us that dragons can be beaten.[27]
>
> G.K. Chesterton
>
> ℬ ℭ

The Emperor's New Clothes, a fable by Hans Christian Andersen, describes an emperor so obsessed with fashionable clothing that he was easily duped by con artists who targeted his vulnerability. The strangers came to his city boasting astonishing skill in weaving fabrics so remarkable that they were invisible to anyone who was either stupid or unfit for his office.

The emperor hired the two men to weave the cloth with mysterious power, even providing the costly silk and gold thread the weavers demanded to begin the work. Day after day, they made a great flourish of weaving at empty looms. When the king sent officials to observe their progress, no one would admit there was nothing on the looms. Instead, fearful that they would be revealed to be stupid or unfit, the king's trusted officials described nonexistent material.

Even the emperor pretended to see spectacular fabrics. He, too, was fearful he'd be deemed unfit if he admitted he couldn't see the enigmatic cloth. The weavers took their deception further, pretending to make clothing for the king from their fascinating cloth. With great fanfare, the emperor was robed in his new garments and taken to parade in front of the people, all who were silenced by the fear that they would be deemed unfit or stupid if they admitted they couldn't see any cloth—or clothing—on their emperor.

The weavers' deception was finally exposed by a little child watching the emperor parade through the town in his nonexistent new garments. "But he hasn't got anything on," the little child said. Only then did everyone realize they had all been hoodwinked.

What type(s) of distorted thinking did the Emperor exhibit? _____

_____

_____

_____

_____

_____

_____

_____

_____

What about the people who remained silent? Were they deluded by cognitive distortions, too? If so, which one(s)? _____

_____

_____

_____

_____

_____

_____

80 CB

All deception in the course of life is indeed nothing else but a lie reduced to practice, and falsehood passing from words into things.[28]

Robert Southey

80 CB

In the classic folk tale, **Little Red Riding Hood,** the protagonist is in the process of doing something helpful and kind—taking a basket of food to her ill grandmother—when she is tricked by a wolf. After Red Riding Hood naively tells the wolf where she is going, he goes there first, to eat her grandmother and take her place.

Red Riding Hood is puzzled by the changes she observes in her "grandmother," stating "What big hands you have!" The wolf disguises his voice, his intent and his plan until Red Riding Hood notices his big teeth. Finally, the wolf's objective is obvious when he responds, "The better to eat you with!"

Review the list of distorted thought patterns. What, if any, types of distorted thinking apply to Little Red Riding Hood's choices? _____

_____

_____

Later in this fable, a hunter comes and rescues both Red Riding Hood and her grandmother from the wolf's stomach. Do you think she might have exhibited **Blaming** cognitive distortions for being duped by the wolf?

_____ Yes _____ No Why? _____

_____

_____

If you can recall the story of Red Riding Hood, describe additional distorted thinking patterns any of the story's other characters exhibit:

_____

_____

_____

Do you think Little Red Riding Hood should blame herself for the wolf's deception? _____ Yes _____ No Do you ever blame yourself for being molested? _____

_____

_____

If you answered "yes" to blaming yourself, describe why—and when, below:

_____

_____

_____

4. Day Four: **Move from Blaming to Aiming** (for New Perspectives)

Predators, like wolves, look for vulnerability in their victims. If you were duped by a sexual predator, the blame is <u>not</u> yours. It belongs to the person

> ໒ ຕ
> _____
>
> We're so sure we'd be happy if only we could get free of our troubles, but going through life without troubles is not an option. While trouble-free times may come, at best they endure briefly... As it turns out, being happy has nothing to do with having trouble or not having it. Rather it's one's attitude toward trouble that makes all the difference. [29]
>
> Mike Mason
>
> _____
> ໒ ຕ

who molested you. Every day you remain in "blame mode" keeps you stuck in the negativity and/or despair of the abuse.

Review the list of cognitive distortions at the beginning of this chapter—notice that "blaming" is one type of distorted thinking. Whether you are blaming yourself or someone else, blaming keeps you focused on the problems instead of solutions. As you continue working through this book, you'll discover new perspectives that can help you experience freedom from the "blame trap" so you will no longer get stuck in the past.

 Explore - *Praise the Lord, O my soul; all my inmost being, praise his holy name. Praise the Lord, O my soul, and forget not all his benefits – who forgives all your sins and heals all your diseases, who redeems your life from the pit and crowns you with love and compassion, who satisfies your desires with good things so that your youth is renewed like the eagle's.*

Psalm 103:1-5, NIV

Note: there can be biological, psychological and spiritual components to depression and/or anxiety. If you are experiencing depression that is so problematic you are unable to do ordinary tasks, make an appointment with your family doctor or a psychiatrist to discuss your concerns.

The following questions can help you ascertain the intensity of your concerns. Place a check [✓] by each of the following areas in which you are currently experiencing concern. If you have been experiencing a loss of interest in your usual activities for at least two weeks and are experiencing four or more of the concerns listed on the next two pages, it is time for you to contact a physician and/or a mental health professional.

[   ] **Sleep**

Approximately how many hours do you sleep each night? _____

How often, if ever, do you wake up in the middle of the night and find yourself unable to return to sleep? _____

Are you experiencing either recurrent insomnia or hypersomnia (excessive daytime sleepiness)? _____ Yes _____ No Explain _____

_____

_____

_____

_____

_____

_____

_____

₧ ₨

Search me [thoroughly], O God, and know my heart! Try me and know my thoughts! And see if there is any wicked or hurtful way in me, and lead me in the way everlasting.

Psalm 139:23-24, AMP

₧ ₨

[   ] Interests

Are you interested in activities that you have enjoyed in the past or have you lost interest in going to work, being with people or doing recreational activities? _____ Yes _____ No Explain _____

_____

_____

_____

[   ] Guilt

Are you feeling guilty about anything or living in a state of constant self-condemnation? _____ Yes _____ No Explain _____

_____

_____

_____

_____

[   ] Energy

Is your energy level about the same as it usually is, or has it increased or decreased in recent weeks or months? _____ Yes _____ No Explain _____

_____

_____

Do you feel unusually fatigued, in a way that isn't due to a medical condition? _____ Yes _____ No Explain _____

_____

_____

_____

_____

[   ] Concentration

Are you able to concentrate? _____ Yes _____ No Explain _____

_____

_____

_____

[   ] Appetite

Has your appetite increased—with resultant weight gain, or decreased—with weight loss? _____ Yes _____ No Explain _____

_____

_____

_____

ജ യ
_____

Consistent, physician-approved exercise and healthful eating are two important considerations for your healing journey.
_____
ജ യ

[   ] **Psychomotor Agitation or Retardation**

Do others notice (on a regular basis) that your movements are either agitated or slowed down? [Agitation could include incoherent conversation, unrestrained gestures, hair twirling and/or pacing. Psychomotor retardation appears as sluggish coordination and/or speech articulation. ___ Yes ___ No

Explain _____

_____

_____

_____

_____

_____

[   ] **Suicide:**

Have you had any thoughts of harming yourself? ____ Yes ____ No

Explain _____

_____

_____

_____

_____

_____

If so, have you thought of how you would kill yourself*? ___ Yes ___ No

Explain _____

_____

_____

_____

_____

_____

*If you answered "Yes," contact a physician or mental health professional immediately.

Anger can also be an indicator of depression. If you have a "short fuse" that is triggered when you have to stand in a seemingly-motionless line at a store, get stuck in traffic, or by a co-worker's habits, pause and notice how long you have felt like this. If many of the statements above apply to you, you might be experiencing depression that looks like anger.

If friends and family, co-workers or acquaintances have attempted to help you deal with challenging emotions and you have resisted their help, perhaps now is the right time to allow yourself to look for a trained professional [i.e. a licensed counselor, pastor, psychiatrist, etc.] who can help with your concerns. Be sure to ask what, if any, experience s/he has in helping people heal from sexual abuse.

ઐ   ૈ

Sing to the Lord! Praise the Lord! For though I was poor and needy, he rescued me from my oppressors.

Jeremiah 20:13, NLT

.ઐ   ૈ

5. Day Five: **Journaling to Freedom & Joy**

Journaling is a superb way to begin experiencing new freedom and joy in your daily life. It is a tangible way to shift your focus from old thought patterns to new ones. Before you can change your focus, though, you need to train yourself to recognize when your thoughts are distorted. You can review the list of cognitive distortions on pages 29 and 30 to get specific ideas. Another way to identify distorted thought patterns is to stop and notice when you are feeling worried, sad, anxious, distressed, fearful or depressed and "think backwards" and wonder about what specific thoughts could be fueling those feelings. [If you feel depressed after you have experienced a loss of a loved one, long-term illness, divorce or another significant loss, you need to allow yourself time to grieve that loss rather than denying or repressing the pain. Grief is not the same as distorted thinking; however, living in grief for years after the loss could move your life into the realm of cognitive distortions. If you are experiencing profound grief, you could read "A Grace Disguised: How the Soul Grows through Loss" by Jerry Sittser, or other excellent books on that subject.]

Distorted thoughts are fed by choosing a negative focus on an event, emotion or failure rather than allowing yourself to rest in God's peace, healing and life. As you recognize specific distorted thoughts, you can resolve to transform your life by changing how you think.

Appendix B has a sample format you can copy and use for your journaling process. Or, you can design your own format in a journal or notebook. It is vital to invest **at least 20 minutes daily journaling** new ways of responding to life. Remember to **date each entry** so you can track your progress. Handwriting your journal entries is a key part of the process; completing this on a computer will **not** be as effective as the process of writing. Below are examples of journaling to help you begin this **three-step process**.

Sample Three-Step Journal Entries:

1. Automatic Negative Thought(s)

   I am never going to have a healthy relationship. I am a loser.

2. Type of Cognitive Distortion(s)

   All or Nothing Thinking; Labeling

3. New Healing Thought(s)

   I can make new choices in how I relate to people. With God's help, I can quit focusing on my past and enjoy the future.

୫୦ ଓଃ

Stop yourself when you feel sad, depressed, anxious, fearful, etc. **Think** "backwards" to discover what thoughts have been in your mind during the last hour(s) or day. **Look** for the thoughts that fuel the emotions you've been experiencing. **Write** down the thoughts you identify as distorted (see the list of cognitive distortions below *or on pages 29-30).*

- Emotional Reasoning
- Jumping to Conclusions
- All or Nothing Thinking
- Should Thinking
- Overgeneralization
- Catastrophizing
- Filtering
- Blaming & Labeling
- Control Myth
- Overlooking the Positive

୫୦ ଓଃ

Week Three - Weekend Bonus Work

The third stage of psychosocial development is Early School Age, which includes ages four to six. At this stage, development occurs through the central process of identification. Identifying with his or her family via positive interactions, a child begins to realize he or she is capable. The child also learns to take the initiative and to feel effective in what he or she does, cultivating a sense of purpose.[30] If this stage isn't successfully completed, guilt or inhibition can occur.

Do you, in general, have a sense of purpose for your life? ـــــــ Yes ـــــــ No

Explain _____

_____

_____

If you were molested at this stage of development, you might feel inhibited when you attempt to interact with others. You might also feel as though you don't have a purpose for living, **but you do**! Consider the following verses.

For I know the thoughts and plans that I have for you, says the Lord, thoughts and plans for welfare and peace and not for evil, to give you hope in your final outcome. Jeremiah 29:11, AMP

For we are God's masterpiece. He has created us anew in Christ Jesus, so we can do the good things he planned for us long ago. Ephesians 2:10, NLT

Gender identification occurs from ages four through six. If you are struggling in this area, it could be because of molestation at this or an earlier stage of development. Other factors could be involved, also.

What was happening in your life from ages four through six? (If you aren't aware of your life at this stage of development and know of safe relatives, you could possibly contact them to help you answer this question.) _____

_____

_____

_____

_____

_____

_____

_____

_____

_____

_____

_____

ଅ ଞ

Many persons have a wrong idea of what constitutes true happiness. It is not attained through self-gratification but through fidelity to a worthy purpose.[31]

Helen Keller

ଅ ଞ

Are We Having FUD Yet?

Chapter Four

The term "FUD" represents "fear, uncertainty and doubt." By this time in the course, you might notice the treacherous FUD trifecta jockeying for your attention.

One acrostic for fear is **"False Evidence Appearing Real."** Are you accepting false evidence regarding your future prospects? _____ Yes _____ No

Think about what you tell yourself about your future and **write it down**: _____

_____

_____

_____

_____

_____

Staying trapped in the frozen emotions of abuse often feels more viable than the hope of living in freedom. You might feel unsure about your progress or question that you can really change. However, as you consciously apply the previous three chapters, change will occur. You can make the determined choice to begin to doubt your doubts instead of believing them. Today, you can move out of the FUD House into new awareness of who you are and what you can do.

The focus this week is **Competence**, one of the five vital areas damaged by sexual abuse. There are times when everyone struggles with feeling incompetent—when passed up for a job promotion or betrayed in a friendship, when a relationship ends or a course seems too difficult to complete.

However, the struggle with competence at the core of one's being is different from circumstantial or relational challenges. It is a sense of being less than others, a belief that one is inherently not as valuable or capable as others of similar education and ability.

Changing this basic core belief about oneself requires replacing a sense of incompetence with a new awareness of one's worth. Many abuse survivors discover that gaining insight into God's love helps them see their own value and competence. The difficulty of this, though, is that it is often difficult for an abuse survivor to be able to trust anyone—especially God.

An inability to trust often is a direct result of the disruption abuse brings to the developmental process. Not being able to trust anyone (even yourself), not feeling worthy, or believing others don't like or respect you can all be the direct result of the sexual abuse you experienced.

ဆၢ ဃ

Who am I, that the Lord of all the earth would care to know my name? Would care to feel my hurt? [32]

Casting Crowns
Who Am I? (Lyrics)

ဆၢ ဃ

It is important to identify the relationship of your emotions to your abuse and to begin to actively choose new beliefs that are not shaped by prior abuse. This week offers specific new ways to gain a sense of self-respect and competence.

Core Healing Goal: to establish new beliefs which result in self-respect and competence.

1. Day One: **Investigating**

   Describe a situation where you have experienced feelings of incompetence.

   _____

   _____

   _____

   Can you recall the first time you sensed this type of emotion? _____

   _____

   _____

   _____

   _____

   Has anyone ever called you names like "stupid," "useless," "blockhead," or "idiot"? _____ Yes _____ No Which name(s) were you called? _____

   _____

   Write down any other demeaning names you remember others calling you.

   _____

   _____

   _____

   _____

   How you would prefer others behave toward you? _____

   _____

   _____

   Circle any names below *you* can use to describe *yourself* that would help you live in *new* ways now.

Hopeful	Capable	Kind	Gracious	Giving
Thoughtful	Caring	God's Child	Beloved	Cherished
Made New	Forgiven	Chosen	Loving	Protected
Comforted	Faithful	Persevering	Determined	Diligent

2. Day Two: **Discovering Truth**

Read **Psalm 139** and find words or phrases describing God's loving design of you. Write down His view of you in the column "God's Opinion of Me." Record your response to God's design of you under "My Opinion of Me."

Verse	God's Opinion of Me	My Opinion of Me

ৰ ৪

For we are God's masterpiece. He has created us anew in Christ Jesus, so we can do the good things he planned for us long ago.

Ephesians 2:10, NLT

ৰ ৪

3. Day Three: **Examining Competency from God's Perspective**

Not that we are competent in ourselves to claim anything for ourselves, but our competence comes from God. He has made us competent as ministers of a new covenant—not of the letter but of the Spirit; for the letter kills, but the Spirit gives life.

2 Corinthians 3:4-6, NIV

Who is an unfailing source for competency/sufficiency/confidence? _____
_____

According to 2 Corinthians 3:4-6, why did God make you competent? _____
_____
_____
_____
_____

According to these verses, the Holy Spirit gives _____

God provides new life, one in which you can walk in grace and mercy: *But because of his great love for us, God, who is rich in mercy, made us alive with Christ even when we were dead in transgressions—it is by grace you have been saved* (Ephesians 2:4,5 NIV). In Him, you can be set free to experience His love and plan for your life. You are a masterpiece created by God to do good works which He has equipped you to do (see Ephesians 2:10).

Consider 2 Corinthians 3:4-6 again. Then describe two ways you can begin living in God's opinion instead of yours: _____
_____
_____
_____
_____
_____
_____

Adam and Eve's rebellion in the Garden of Eden unleashed evil that has impacted all of creation. Since sin and death entered the world, life as God intended it has never been the same. Sexual abuse is one horrific consequence of human sin, which was never part of God's loving design for His creation.

Terrible things happened to you, yet God's plan for you now—and for your future—is good. Your past cannot destroy your future—unless you choose to let it define you. Today, you can begin to trust God rather than live in past fears and doubts. God didn't abandon you or cause your hurt. Instead, He sent His only Son to earth to give you new life and the strength to live it.

Write down any doubts you have about your current ability to live in freedom and hope:

_____

_____

_____

_____

_____

_____

_____

_____

_____

Are you willing to entrust your doubts to God and to begin to doubt them instead of doubting God? _____ Yes _____ No Why? _____

_____

_____

_____

_____

_____

_____

4. Day Four: **Living in Competence Today**

God promises to restore your soul, to renew your strength and hope.

In Psalm 23 (NLT), King David describes these promises:

The Lord is my shepherd; I have all that I need. He lets me rest in green meadows; he leads me beside peaceful streams. He renews my strength. He guides me along right paths, bringing honor to his name. Even when I walk through the darkest valley, I will not be afraid, for you are close beside me. Your rod and your staff protect and comfort me. You prepare a feast for me in the presence of my enemies. You honor me by anointing my head with oil. My cup overflows with blessings. Surely your goodness and unfailing love will pursue me all the days of my life, and I will live in the house of the Lord forever.

As you read and consider Psalm 23, imagine God as your Shepherd. (Often survivors of abuse have difficulty viewing God as Father because a

I remember my affliction and my wandering, the bitterness and the gall. I well remember them, and my soul is downcast within me.

Yet this I call to mind and therefore I have hope: Because of the Lord's great love we are not consumed, for his compassions never fail. They are new every morning; great is your faithfulness.

Lamentations 3:19-23, NIV

father-figure molested them; it might be helpful at this point to switch your perspective of God to the Good Shepherd until you feel safe seeing Him as your heavenly Father.) A Good Shepherd protects his sheep and makes sure they have a safe place to live. In fact, a worthy shepherd makes sure his sheep have absolutely everything they need. What do you notice in the above psalm about your Good Shepherd's promise to care for you today?

_____

_____

_____

_____

Your Shepherd wants to accomplish His magnificent design for your life, but He will not force you either to change or grow. He waits for you to allow Him to help you heal.

 Explore - *"But all who devour you will be devoured; all your enemies will go into exile. Those who plunder you will be plundered; all who make spoil of you I will despoil. But I will restore you to health and heal your wounds", declares the Lord, "because you are called an outcast, Zion for whom no one cares."*

Jeremiah 30:16-17, NIV

Nevertheless, I will bring health and healing to it; I will heal my people and will let them enjoy abundant peace and security.

Jeremiah 33:6, NIV

The Lord will accomplish what concerns me; Your lovingkindness, O Lord, is everlasting; Do not forsake the works of Your hands.

Psalm 138:8, NASU

For we are his workmanship, created in Christ Jesus for good works, which God prepared beforehand, that we should walk in them.

Ephesians 2:10, ESV

As you consider God's promises (above), imagine what your healing could look like. Take time now to write a note to God, thanking Him that He wants to heal your wounds.

_____

_____

_____

_____

_____

_____

_____

ઈ ⅏

When we put our cares in His hands, He puts His peace in our hearts. [34]

Author Unknown

ઈ ⅏

5. Day Five: **Journaling to Freedom & Joy**

Continue your journaling focusing on how **Competence** is being developed in your life. Journaling is a superb way to experience joy and freedom each day. It is a tangible way to shift your focus from old thought patterns to new ones.

Appendix B has a sample format you can copy and use for your journaling process. Or, you can design your own format in a journal or notebook. It is vital to invest **at least 20 minutes daily journaling** new ways of responding to life. Remember to **date each entry** so you can track your progress. Handwriting your journal entries is a key part of the process; completing this on a computer will **not** be as effective as the process of writing. Below are examples of journaling to help you begin this **three-step process**.

Sample journal entries using **COMPETENCE** as the focus.

1. Automatic Negative Thought(s)

   I feel inferior to others when I walk into a room. I feel like everyone else is OK... and I'm not.

2. Type of Cognitive Distortion(s)

   Emotional Reasoning; Jumping to conclusions

3. New Healing Thought(s)

   Thinking about Psalm 23, I am making a new choice (even though I don't feel it yet) to believe I can enjoy God's goodness and overflowing love. Doing that, I realize I am not inferior to anyone else. God has an original, GOOD, plan for my life!

ઠ૦ ૦ૐ

I have strength for all things in Christ Who empowers me [I am ready for anything and equal to anything through Him Who infuses inner strength into me; I am self-sufficient in Christ's sufficiency].

Philippians 4:13, AMP

ઠ૦ ૦ૐ

Week Four - Weekend Bonus Work

The fourth stage of psychosocial development is Middle Childhood, which includes ages six to twelve. At this stage, development occurs through the central process of education. A child will typically be industrious at school, developing a sense of competence, unless some sort of developmental disruption occurs.[35]

If molestation occurs at this stage of development—or if it occurred in prior stages of development, a child often feels inferior to others. Instead of making friends and becoming part of team play, a child might seem apathetic or disinterested in what other children are doing.

If this developmental stage isn't successfully completed, an ongoing, problematic self-consciousness can be a downside of disrupted development. In some children, violent and/or bullying behaviors accompany the sense of powerlessness produced in them by their perpetrator(s) of sexual abuse.

As you can see, there aren't simple explanations surrounding the complex emotions experienced by survivors of sexual molestation. As you read about this stage of development, imagine yourself back at an age between six and twelve.

What age did you choose to imagine? _____ Now, picture Jesus, your loving Shepherd there with you. Imagine love and acceptance in His eyes and tenderness in His voice. What is He saying to you? _____

_____

_____

_____

_____

Relax, close your eyes and breathe deeply, inhaling through your nose. Count to 4, 5, or 6 (whatever is comfortable for you), allowing your lungs to inflate as you inhale. (Be sure you inhale deeply enough to engage your diaphragm.) Breathe out through your mouth, emptying your lungs as you exhale. (It might help to picture your lungs like two balloons; as you inhale, inflate your lungs; as you exhale, empty them.) Continue breathing, allowing yourself to relax fully, imagining you are safe in Your Shepherd's love. Describe your experience below.

_____

_____

_____

_____

_____

_____

ᙇ ᙈ

Nowhere does the Bible exhort us to do anything in our own strength, but only in the Lord. It would be cruel to expect anyone to be always happy apart from God. But "in the Lord"—why not: Who wouldn't be overjoyed with a God who "has given us everything we need for life and godliness" (2 Peter 1:3)? [36]

Mike Mason

ᙇ ᙈ

Name Your Tyrant

Chapter Five

The focus of this chapter is **Security**, which indicates being safe and protected within a sanctuary or safe haven of some kind. A safe haven could be a tangible place like a house, an intellectual realization, a spiritual sense of comfort and peace, or an emotional context, such as a relationship.

"Home" is many people's description of a secure, safe place, but "home" is not a secure place for people who have been abused within its walls. Insecurity, the opposite of security, suggests a lack of safety and/or a general feeling of instability, unpredictability, anxiety, uncertainty or fear.

As you read the preceding description of "security" and "insecurity," do you notice any words or phrases in the paragraphs that relate to your life? As you note them below, please add additional words or phrases to describe your experience of security and insecurity.

Security: _____

_____

_____

_____

Insecurity: _____

_____

_____

_____

ဆ

The name of the Lord is a strong tower; the righteous run to it and are safe.
Proverbs 18:10, NKJV

Because sexual abuse generates complex physical, emotional, mental, social and spiritual harm, its survivors often feel unsafe and unprotected long after the abuse ends. The child or adult who has been sexually abused—whether by inappropriate touch, violent molestation, exposure to pornography or nudity, or by any other form of sexual abuse—has been under someone else's control. This week's work is designed to help you become aware of ways in which you could still be experiencing negative influences from past abuse.

In this chapter, a sexual predator is referred to as a tyrant or dictator. Like a tyrant, a perpetrator of sexual abuse is someone who takes control over someone else. Many survivors live as though dominated by their abuser for years or even decades after the abuse stops. It is an essential part of your healing process to "name your tyrant" by determining how current thinking, feeling and actions are triggered by past sexual assault.

Core Healing Goal: to move from attitudes or actions shaped by abuse into the safety and security God provides by making healing choices each day.

1. Day One: **From Insecurity to Security**

Insecurity can feel like anxiety and breeds self-doubt and uncertainty. . If your past continues to create feelings of self-doubt, it is important to recognize those feelings so you can move out from under their control.

Rank the following statements using a scale of 0 to 10, with 0 being "neutral or none" and 10 being "as much as I can imagine."

_____ When I'm feeling insecure, I look for people who will show me love and affection. But I always feel like either they can't get it right or I can't. I still feel unloved.

_____ When I'm stressed I turn to alcohol, drugs, food, or _____ (circle your answer), as a means of coping with the situation.

_____ I am not able to set boundaries and people take advantage of me.

_____ When I feel rejected, I turn my anger inward and withdraw.

_____ I don't feel safe anywhere.

_____ I try to be perfect so other people will like me.

_____ My insecurity often expresses itself as anger.

_____ When I'm in a group, I am afraid to speak; I know I'll say or do something stupid.

_____ No one would listen to me when I was being molested; no one will help me now.

_____ If you ranked the majority of your answers as "6" or higher, please describe your concerns to a counselor, physician, pastor, priest, rabbi or other professional trained in helping people who have been sexually abused.

What circumstances, people or events trigger insecurities in you now? _____

_____

_____

_____

_____

When you walk into a room, do you feel confident or do you feel hesitant, wondering whether you'll say or do the "right" thing? Explain: _____

_____

_____

_____

_____

_____

_____

୫୦ ଓଃ

If you look at the world, you'll be distressed. If you look within, you'll be depressed. If you look at God you'll be at rest.[37]

Corrie Ten Boom

୫୦ ଓଃ

Think about your relationships and interactions at work or home. Describe what might change if you felt safe in everyday life: _____

_____

_____

_____

_____

 Explore - Though your past can't be changed, it doesn't have to dictate your present or your future. Your present and future will be shaped by what you choose to believe now.

He who dwells in the shelter of the Most High will rest in the shadow of the Almighty. I will say of the Lord, "He is my refuge and my fortress, my God, in whom I trust." Surely he will save you from the fowler's snare and from the deadly pestilence. He will cover you with his feathers, and under his wings you will find refuge; his faithfulness will be your shield and rampart. You will not fear the terror of night, nor the arrow that flies by day, nor the pestilence that stalks in the darkness, nor the plague that destroys at midday.

Psalm 91:1-6, NIV

Write down key words or phrases from this Psalm that portray the security that can be yours for the rest of your life: _____

_____

_____

_____

_____

2. Day Two: **ID Your Tyrant**

At its essence, sexual abuse is about power and control—not about love and certainly not about healthy sexuality. When you were molested, you likely felt powerless. Most survivors couldn't stop the people who abused their bodies and lied about what was happening. One problem of living in a tyrant's lies is that they can become a person's "normal." If that was your life, you likely learned to rationalize what was happening in order to survive. Every time you rationalized, you inexplicably learned to believe "rational lies." The lies of the past can keep you trapped and feeling unsafe in the present.

Some perpetrators say things like, "What we are doing is our secret. If you tell anyone, I'll hurt [your dog, cat, brother, mother, friend, etc.]." Some children have been told, "Your mom will divorce me if you tell her about this—and it will be your fault." Since a child's brain cannot sift through the lies of abuse, the result is often that the victim believes the perpetrator when he or she says that the molestation is the child's fault. The child often lives in constant terror that s/he could cause harm to someone else. Often children suffer molestation for years to protect a sibling from their tormentor.

When a perpetrator of sexual abuse says something like, "This is only tickling. Everybody loves to be tickled," and won't listen when a child protests, the child learns to feel helpless and quits trying to object to what is happening. Teenagers report being told, "You know you wanted it," after they have been manipulated to do something that leaves them feeling alone, empty, and robbed.

Your perpetrator may have told you it was a "game" or that it was "OK because this is how to be a grown-up." Some sexual abusers even tell their victims "this is the mommy and daddy game." How perplexing for a child to be told that something so confusing—and often painful—is "good."

The good news for you today is this—you can learn a completely different way of thinking and living now that will free you from what happened then. Moving away from the lies of sexual abuse is challenging because of the incredible confusion already delivered to your mind, body and soul. A child's mind cannot comprehend when a person he or she should be able to trust is saying something is "good" when it feels anything but that. Another type of confusion is experienced by children when the only time they are told they are "special" is when their bodies are used for someone's selfish sexual gratification. A person who once seemed safe proved he or she is not safe at all.

You can terminate your abuser's lies by consciously choosing not to believe them in your mind, emotions, soul or behavior. First, though, you'll need to bring the lies to the surface so you can replace them with Truth.

Write down any "rational lies" from your past that are hindering your sense of safety now: _____

_____

_____

_____

_____

_____

To get a small sense of the massive inner erosion caused by sexual abuse, think about a child who is told that pink, yellow, and blue paper play money is real money. S/he might see people paying for things with a different kind of money—green paper bills—and still believe the lie she has been told—because it was someone she should be able to trust who told her real things can be bought with the money that came in a game box.

> ᔕᗝ ᑕᗷ
>
> **The good news for you today is this—you can learn a completely different way of thinking and living now that will free you from what happened then.**
>
> ᔕᗝ ᑕᗷ

Imagine the same child at age six, trying to pay for school lunch with play money. She would be confused when her classmates laughed. Though ultimately she'd figure out she had been duped, the trauma of being tricked into spending play money would leave her with a lack confidence, a sense of insecurity.

Indescribable confusion emerges because the body God created to experience sexual pleasure in marriage didn't know how to "shut down" when your perpetrator touched you and told you it was "good." On the one hand, some part of a child's body might have felt good; on the other hand, he or she felt horrible. Even while being raped, women can experience orgasm, which can result in years of bewilderment about what really happened. You can know rape is rape; it is a violent crime, whether any part of it felt "good" or not. If your perpetrator molested you repeatedly, you might think you didn't resist him enough for it to be called rape. Sadly, a survivor of sexual abuse is groomed to act powerless after being threatened with dire consequences for resistance.

Catastrophic, staggering insecurity is fostered when a child or an adult is out of control of his or her own body! Ordinary things, like feeling safe in bed at night, are not possible for a child who is molested when he or she tries to sleep. A child whose predator is a family member, teacher, family friend or club leader develops intangible fears about being with people. Sometimes the fears are so overwhelming that, by adulthood, "numbing-out behaviors"— like substance abuse, constant activity, eating disorders, sexual acting-out or other obsessions become a part of daily life used to silence hidden pain. Survivors of sexual abuse often have numbed out their emotions so thoroughly that they are "frozen," with an inability to feel a normal range of human emotions like love, sadness, hope, peace, joy, etc.

Can you think of anything you are doing or have done to silence the pain of your abuse? _____

_____

_____

_____

_____

Many abuse survivors are hushed by family members who demand, "Don't ever tell anyone!" when they find out about the molestation. Others are accused of lying about what happened. Still others are not heard when they try to tell someone what happened to them. That forced silence increases the survivor's pain and feelings of worthlessness. When the one who tells a child or teenager *not to tell* is someone who should be protecting that person, additional confusion and hopelessness ensue. Sometimes the adults who say "don't tell" are survivors of abuse who never dealt with the pain in their own lives.

⋈

A child whose predator is a family member, teacher, family friend or club leader develops intangible fears about being with people.

⋈

What, if anything, did people do or say to keep you silent? _____

_____

_____

_____

_____

_____

Your silence can end now, whether it was caused by numbing your emotions or demanded by others who didn't hear, care or understand your pain. You can tell a trusted counselor, pastor, rabbi, friend or law enforcement officer. And you can open your heart to God as the Shepherd who cares and hears you when you cry. The psalmist understood needing someone to care when he wrote:

 Explore - *I look for someone to come and help me, but no one gives me a passing thought! No one will help me; no one cares a bit what happens to me. Then I pray to you, O Lord. I say, "You are my place of refuge. You are all I really want in life. Hear my cry, for I am very low. Rescue me from my persecutors, for they are too strong for me. Bring me out of prison so I can thank you. The godly will crowd around me, for you are good to me.*

Psalm 142:4-7, NLT

A vital step to eliminating the obstacles to your well-being is to repeatedly remind yourself, "I am no longer in that situation." [**If you are currently in an abusive situation**, please **call** your **local police** or **800.96ABUSE** (800.962.2873) as soon as you are in a safe place where your call won't be overheard by your abuser.]

Will you make the choice to stop shutting out or numbing emotions (sorrow, fear, hurt, etc.) with activities, alcohol, drugs, inappropriate sexuality, etc.? Will you entrust your sorrow to God and begin to believe in His gift of hope and healing? _____ Yes _____ No

If your answer is "Yes," explain when and how. If "No," explain what is holding you back from making this critical decision.

_____

_____

_____

_____

_____

_____

_____

Satan, the ultimate Mr. Unclean, hates that mortal creatures have been made clean through the grace of Calvary and the sanctifying work of the Holy Spirit. If he can't make us unclean, he will at least do everything he can to make us *feel* unclean.[39]

Beth Moore

Today, you can step out of the insecurity of your past into a safe, secure and free future. You can allow God to heal the pain of abuse so there is no longer a need to "anesthetize" any area of your life. A vital part of your healing journey is to choose to live in this moment, today, not in the past. As you recognize areas of core damage, you can move forward. You can allow your new awareness to be a catalyst for growth rather than an excuse to stay trapped in the pain of the past.

During your healing process, you might experience discomfort as emotions "thaw." Rather than letting the discomfort stop your progress, simply notice what you are feeling and continue applying what you are learning in your daily life. In other words, feeling some pain is OK. It is simply an indication that you are growing! [If your pain is so great you aren't able to function at home, work, school, etc., please obtain professional help immediately.]

3. Day Three: **New Choices, Not Old Tyrants**

Think about the root issues which could fuel insecurity in your day-to-day life and write them down below so you can be alert to their subtle influence. Old "tyrants" from the past could be fear of talking to people, believing you'll never get "it" right, feeling like you will always be hurt by others, etc. Listen carefully to your self-talk, noticing any automatic negative thoughts that deliver discouraging messages. [At this point, if you're unsure about how to identify negative automatic thoughts, turn back to chapter three and review the ten basic types of distorted thinking. You can also turn to Appendix A to learn how to replace distorted thought patterns with biblical perspectives.]

What "dictators" are you experiencing today? _____
_____
_____

From your past? _____
_____
_____

At work? _____
_____
_____

At home? _____
_____
_____

ജ ര

Cruelty is a tyrant that's always attended with fear. [40]

Thomas Fuller

ജ ര

With friends? _____

_____

_____

Other situations/areas of concern: _____

_____

_____

_____

_____

Review the "tyrants" you named and be alert for their presence in your thoughts and feelings. When you notice any of them creeping into your daily life, you can kick them out! Whatever "has" your mind "has" you; thus it is vital to choose what you think, making consciously healthy choices for your present and your future.

When a survivor of sexual molestation numbs emotions during and following abuse, it is because it was too painful to experience the complex emotional, physical, spiritual and mental agony. No one is designed to go through the utter disrespect of having his or her body used by someone else. Your trauma may have been so horrific that your mind continues "numbing out," shutting out memories of what happened because you cannot find a rational explanation for your experiences. Instead of looking for a rational explanation for a criminal act, you can choose to experience positive emotions now, realizing that "numbing" memories is no longer helpful. Instead of "freezing" painful past emotions, you can experience positive emotions, by consciously living in the present.

It takes determination to move into freedom. Before you are able to trust God and accept His freedom, you might need to remind yourself that it was not God who caused you to experience sexual abuse. He gave people the amazing freedom to choose their thoughts, attitudes and actions. Sadly, many abuse that freedom and choose damaging, destructive behaviors that have horrific consequences in their own and others' lives. The good news is that others' choices do not have to determine your choices. Today, you can follow your loving Shepherd instead of being tyrannized by anyone or anything. You can move from being a "survivor" of sexual abuse to being someone who thrives, someone who experiences growth in every area of life.

 Explore - *You answer us with awe-inspiring acts done in righteousness, O God, our savior, the hope of all the ends of the earth and of the most distant sea, the one who set the mountains in place with his strength, the one who is clothed with power, ...You crown the year with your goodness, and richness overflows wherever you are. The pastures in the desert overflow with richness. The hills are surrounded with joy.*

Psalm 65:5-6,11-12, NIV

ಬ ಚ

The ultimate tyrant is Satan, who Jesus refers to as a thief in the verse below.

The thief comes only to steal and kill and destroy; I came that they may have life, and have it abundantly.

John 10:10, NASU

ಬ ಚ

What things from your past do you need to let go of now? _____

_____

_____

_____

_____

_____

_____

_____

_____

It might seem impossible to move from insecurity to security—but you can do it, in God's strength. The following verses offer practical ways to learn how to feel secure.

 Explore - *The world is unprincipled. It's dog-eat-dog out there! The world doesn't fight fair. But we don't live or fight our battles that way — never have and never will. The tools of our trade aren't for marketing or manipulation, but they are for demolishing that entire massively corrupt culture. We use our powerful God-tools for smashing warped philosophies, tearing down barriers erected against the truth of God, fitting every loose thought and emotion and impulse into the structure of life shaped by Christ.*

2 Corinthians 10:3-5 (THE MESSAGE).

Write down two ways you can use the "tools of our trade" described in 2 Corinthians 10:3-5: _____

_____

_____

_____

_____

_____

_____

_____

4. Day Four: **A New Way of Living**

How many years have you been under a "tyrant's" emotional control? _____

Moving away from tyranny is challenging because of how it generated past fear, apathy, discouragement, confusion, anxiety and (name other emotions

        ℰ℧ ℃ℬ
_____

And suddenly all of it's behind you
And I'm here to remind you
That yesterday is gone so wave goodbye
And finally the skies open around you
And love has truly found you
Now everything is alive [41]

Toby Mac
Suddenly (Lyrics)
_____

        ℰ℧ ℃ℛ

you experience in relationship to abuse). _____

_____

_____.

You can face the challenge by relying on God's strength.

Who can snatch the plunder of war from the hands of a warrior? Who can demand that a tyrant let his captives go? But the LORD SAYS, The captives of warriors will be released, and the plunder of tyrants will be retrieved. For I will fight those who fight you, and I will save your children. Isaiah 49:24-25, NLT

Jesus offers hope and freedom instead of tyranny. He says, "*Come to Me, all who are weary and heavy-laden, and I will give you rest. Take My yoke upon you and learn from Me, for I am gentle and humble in heart, and YOU WILL FIND REST FOR YOUR SOULS. For My yoke is easy and My burden is light*" (Matthew 11:28-30, NASU).

What would change in your life today if you rely on God to give you the security and rest He promises? _____

_____

_____

_____

_____

_____

Does it comfort you to know that Jesus understands? ____ Yes ____ No

Explain: _____

_____

_____

_____

You answer us with awe-inspiring acts done in righteousness, O God, our savior, the hope of all the ends of the earth and of the most distant sea, the one who set the mountains in place with his strength, the one who is clothed with power, the one who calms the roar of the seas, their crashing waves, and the uproar of the nations.

You crown the year with your goodness, and richness overflows wherever you are. The pastures in the desert overflow with richness. The hills are surrounded with joy. The pastures are covered with flocks. The valleys are carpeted with grain. All of them shout triumphantly. Indeed, they sing.

Psalm 65:5-6,11-13 GW

As you rely on the facts of God's Word, His faithfulness, and His strength, you can move from insecurity to security, from fear of the past to safety in the present. There are no "tyrants" in God's presence.

CB

_____

Look to Me [Jesus] continually for help, comfort, and companion-ship. Because I am always by your side, the briefest glance can connect you with Me. When you look to Me for help, it flows freely from My Presence. [42]

Sarah Young

_____

ഉ CB

The Bible describes an amazing alternative to the insecurity and fear fueled by abuse.

 Explore - *For as many as are the promises of God, they all find their Yes [answer] in Him [Christ]. For this reason we also utter the Amen (so be it) to God through Him [in His Person and by His agency] to the glory of God. But it is God Who confirms and makes us steadfast and establishes us [in joint fellowship] with you in Christ, and has consecrated and anointed us [enduing us with the gifts of the Holy Spirit]; [He has also appropriated and acknowledged us as His by] putting His seal upon us and giving us His [Holy] Spirit in our hearts as the security deposit and guarantee [of the fulfillment of His promise].*

2 Corinthians 1:20-22, Amplified

The passage above portrays God making His children "steadfast," with the Holy Spirit in their hearts as a guarantee that He will fulfill His promises. What could change in your life if you accept this promise from God as your own? _____

_____

_____

_____

5. Day Five: **Journaling to Freedom & Joy**

Continue your journaling focusing on how **Security** is being developed in your life. Journaling is a superb way to experience joy and freedom each day. It is a tangible way to shift your focus from old thought patterns to new ones. Look for ways to shift your focus from damaging old thoughts to healing new thoughts that help you feel safe and secure. Below are examples of a three-step journaling process.

> Appendix B has a sample format you can copy and use for your journaling process. Or, you can design your own format in a journal or notebook. It is vital to invest **at least 20 minutes daily journaling** new ways of responding to life. Remember to **date each entry** so you can track your progress. Handwriting your journal entries is a key part of the process; completing this on a computer will **not** be as effective as the process of writing. Below are examples of journaling to help you begin this **three-step process**.

Sample Journal using **SECURITY** as the focus.

1. Automatic Negative Thought

This core healing stuff might work for someone else, but it doesn't work for me. What I experienced is worse than anything anyone else did, So how can I ever feel safe? This is a stupid exercise.

And God is able to make all grace abound to you, so that in all things at all times, having all that you need, you will abound in every good work.

2 Corinthians 9:8, NIV

---

2. Type of Cognitive Distortion

Catastrophizing; also (possibly) Blaming and Labeling

3. New Healing Thought(s)

Being stuck in the past gets me nowhere. And comparing myself to other people doesn't help me experience God's promises for my life, either! Whenever I compare myself to other people, I either feel a) inferior to them or b) superior to them. (And I don't want to live in either a self-critical or arrogant mode!). I can make the choice to come to Jesus for safety. Even though I don't feel it yet, I will trust God to give me rest in MY soul, just like He promised to do in Matthew 11:28-30. These two versions of that passage encourage me:

"Come to me, all you who are weary and burdened, and I will give you rest... I am gentle and humble in heart, and you will find rest for your souls." Matthew 11:28-30, NIV

"Are you tired? Worn out? Burned out on religion? Come to me. Get away with me and you'll recover your life. I'll show you how to take a real rest. Walk with me and work with me — watch how I do it. Learn the unforced rhythms of grace. I won't lay anything heavy or ill-fitting on you. Keep company with me and you'll learn to live freely and lightly." Matthew 11:28-30, The Message

OK, I am going to come to Jesus and let Him recover my life. I need the "real rest" He promises. I want to learn to live freely and lightly. I will trust Him to take me away from the emotional pain and tyranny of my past.

> ෨ ෬
>
> So many problems can be solved by being honest about who we are. So many problems, once we release our fears, aren't problems at all.[43]
>
> Melody Beattie
>
> ෨ ෬

Week Five - Weekend Bonus Work

 The fifth stage of psychosocial development is Early Adolescence, which includes ages twelve through eighteen. Development in Early Adolescence occurs through the central process of peer pressure. A preteen or teenager going through this stage naturally cares about what his or her peers think. Those who have been sexually abused tend to care too much about what their friends think, focusing too much on gaining their approval.[44]

This is the stage at which emotional development seems to be on a fast track. Conversely, the person who was molested during or prior to this stage may have significant difficulty managing his or her emotions. Instead of learning to identify with a group, the survivor of molestation might become alienated from peers and/or family.

At this stage, developing loyalty is an aspect of healthy emotional, social, physical and mental development. If development is disrupted, an adolescent could dissociate, which could look like apathy, a lack of feeling, or being unaware of one's surroundings.

Healthy development from ages 12 to 18 includes developing ideals, reasoning ability, and having a positive sense of identity. Possible effects of sexual abuse during this developmental stage include the individual choosing risky behavior, sexually-acting-out, or overemphasis on outward appearance. Some survivors begin using drugs and alcohol to numb the emotional pain fueled by sexual abuse.

Eating disorders can be triggered by numerous factors, one of which could be molestation. When problems are internalized, some individuals develop disorders such as anorexia nervosa, binge eating disorder or bulimia nervosa, possibly in an attempt to exert some control over their own bodies. Eating disorders involve a complex internal process of turning anger, fear, hurt, anxiety, frustration, etc. inward.

If you are experiencing an eating disorder for any reason, please find someone trained in working with them as soon as possible. One place to look is the International Association of Eating Disorder Professionals (IAEDP); another is the American Association of Christian Counselors (AACC), at www.aacc.net; you can link to their "Find a Counselor" section to find someone proficient in helping with eating disorders.

Whether your abuse was during this stage of development or during a prior stage, you may have experienced some repercussions of disrupted development described above. The good news is that you can move away from the disruptions and into a new life.

So if the Son sets you free, you are free through and through.

John 8:36,
THE MESSAGE

59

Think about specific choices you can make today to live with a sense of safety, based not on lies from your past, but on the truth that your life matters now! You can choose to look at today—and tomorrow—with hope based on Truth rather than the lies that might have blinded you to hope before.

After her mother died of complications related to AIDS, Liz Murray was homeless in the spring of 1997. She spent her days picturing herself in school, "participating in classroom discussions and diligently taking notes." She eventually found a high school she describes as "my one yes in a world filled with no." From there she went to Harvard University. She says "it's been up to me to choose a life that measures up to [my] dreams. To get there, the focus has not been on freedom from want but on a clear vision for my life...at the heart of it all was my willingness to be grateful for the things that I already have rather than dwelling on what I don't."[45]

 Explore - *Summing it all up, friends, I'd say you'll do best by filling your minds and meditating on things true, noble, reputable, authentic, compelling, gracious – the best, not the worst; the beautiful, not the ugly; things to praise, not things to curse.*

Philippians 4:8, THE MESSAGE

From Philippians 4:8, list positive things you can choose to think about and briefly explain how you will do it.

_____

_____

_____

_____

_____

_____

_____

_____

_____

_____

_____

_____

_____

_____

_____

_____

ဆ ၄

And though this world, with devils filled, should threaten to undo us, we will not fear, for God hath willed his truth to triumph through us. The Prince of Dark- ness grim, we tremble not for him; his rage we can endure, for lo, his doom is sure; one little word shall fell him.[46]

Martin Luther
A Mighty Fortress is Our God (Lyrics)

ဆ ၄

60

Forgive, Forget and Move On?

Chapter Six

Many survivors are tormented by the idea of forgiveness, feeling brutalized after being told, "You have to forgive, forget and move on. You shouldn't feel like you do." Before we can begin to consider the next core area, Identity, it is important to recognize what forgiveness is—and what it is not. Anyone who demanded that you quickly "forgive, forget and move on" did not understand the nature of healing from sexual abuse. Yes, forgiveness is possible—and essential to your healing—but if you equate forgiving with being able to completely "forget," you could remain unnecessarily stuck in past trauma.

When you "Named Your Tyrant" in chapter five, you might have experienced emotions you haven't felt before. If you have previously denied the extent or ramifications of your abuse, repressed feelings of sadness, horror, anxiety or fear could have surfaced. You might have remembered events from your past you hoped were forever forgotten. If you felt like your suffering didn't matter to anyone, the last chapter was undoubtedly a difficult one.

This chapter is designed to give you relief from the burdens of your past so you can see not only that your experience matters; you can understand how to enjoy new emotions that are not shaped by your past abuse.

Core Healing Goal: to understand what forgiveness is and is not.

1. Day One: **What Forgiveness Is NOT**

   Has anyone told you "You have to forgive, forget and move on"? What was your response? _____

   _____

   _____

   _____

   _____

   Please describe any difficulties you have had in regard to previous attempts at forgiving, forgetting or moving beyond your molestation: _____

   _____

   _____

   _____

   _____

   _____

   _____

          ℰℴ ℭℛ

I have often said, "I forgive you," but even as I said these words my heart remained angry and resentful. I still wanted to hear the story that tells me that I was right after all; I still wanted to hear apologies and excuses; I still wanted the satisfaction of receiving some praise in return – if only the praise for being so forgiving![47]

Henri Nouwen, *Return of the Prodigal Son: A Story of Homecoming*

          ℰℴ ℭℛ

Forgiveness is not forgetting. Though you can learn to forgive, there are many reasons you can't "forget" what happened. One of them has to do with how your brain works. Memories stored there can be triggered by smells, even odors you weren't aware you noticed while you were being abused. Memories can also be prompted by sounds or images—like a voice, face or clothing similar to that belonging to your abuser.

At times, you might feel a sense of dread and not know why. Your senses of touch and taste can also cause you to remember, even when you don't have conscious memories of all that transpired in your past. Like a muscle's reflex actions, your subconscious can trigger conscious memories of the past even when you don't want to go there.

Since beginning your healing journey, you might have experienced intrusive memories, persistent unwanted recollections of horrific past trauma that have possibly been repressed in your subconscious for months, years or decades. Therefore, the idea of "forgetting" presents an impossible goal.

The physiological reality is that it is impossible to entirely "forget." At the same time, it is entirely possible to forgive, which we will continue to explore in this chapter and the next.

Forgiveness is not "understanding" your abuse. Many people erroneously believe they can somehow make sense of the horrors of sexual abuse and that after they do that, they can forgive. This mistaken belief can delay the forgiveness process for so long that it never begins. It is important to look at the challenges of forgiveness with a sense that something better lies beyond those challenges. They are only obstacles that hinder your progress; they do not have the power to keep you "stuck" unless you let them.

> ❧ ❧
>
> It is important to look at the challenges of forgiveness with a sense that there is something better than the challenges. They are only obstacles that hinder your progress; they do not have the power to keep you "stuck" unless you let them.
>
> ❧ ❧

Think about it. Is there really any way you can wrap your mind around the evil inherent in sexual abuse? Is there any way you can truly understand the brutality of someone who intentionally overpowers another human being, wounding so deeply that the core of that person is savagely, yet invisibly, damaged?

Holocaust survivor Elie Wiesel experienced horrifying evil when imprisoned by the Nazis at Auschwitz. He said, "Sometimes I am asked if I know 'the response to Auschwitz'; I answer that not only do I not know it, but that I don't even know if a tragedy of this magnitude *has* a response. What I do know is that there is 'response' in responsibility. When we speak of this era of evil and darkness, so close and yet so distant, 'responsibility' is the key word."[48]

Notice what you are thinking and feeling. Ask God to help you as you consider how to forgive—and who to forgive. Pause to wonder if forgiving your offenders could be your response to Christ's sacrificial love.

While your abuse was happening, how did you feel toward your perpetrator? Circle all applicable words or phrases.

Confused	Afraid	Hopeless	Numb	Defeated
Worried	Helpless	Hurt	Sad	Scared
Paralyzed	Weak	Calm	Angry	Shocked
Vulnerable	Defenseless	Guilty	Terrified	Understood
Trusting	Cheated	Excited	Destroyed	Nervous
Intimidated	Needed to rescue him/her		Needed to protect him/her	

Add other feelings not listed above.

_____

_____

_____

_____

_____

A wide range of emotions is represented in the descriptions above. Review the feelings you circled or added to the list and consider whether you want the emotions of the past to define your future. What do you think? _____

_____

_____

_____

_____

_____

_____

_____

_____

2. Day Two: **One Person's Journey to Forgiveness**

When Elizabeth learned I was writing about forgiveness, she asked to share her story. Elizabeth is a lovely single mom whose trauma began in early childhood. Beginning below through page 67, Elizabeth tells her story in her own words:

When I was born my father went to prison for five years so my mom was left to care for my two-year old brother and me. My mother had endured sexual and physical abuse throughout her life and as a result turned to men and drugs to numb her pain. Due to my mother's drug use and poor choices with men, my childhood was filled with fear. My father got out of prison when I was five and took custody of my brother. He tried to get me to go but I was too afraid that something would happen to my mom if I left her. I felt it was my job to take care of her.

> In the final analysis, forgiveness is an act of faith. It is the belief that God can take care of the fairness problems. It is not fair just to pretend that something doesn't happen. It did happen. It still hurts. It still stings. Forgiveness is not fair, but forgiveness is a way of taking that burden from us and giving it to God who is fair.[49]
>
> Philip Yancey

63

My mom went from one abusive relationship to the next. As a result, we moved several times. I experienced a number of traumatic events. It seemed like the cops were always at our house. The men my mom chose were drug dealers and abusive. I remember going to school and just being so fearful that something was going to happen. I was very withdrawn and isolated.

I was probably around five or six when I was first introduced to sex. I was sitting in the backseat of my mom's car. Some guy was driving and my mom was in the passenger seat. I don't remember much except them being drunk and my mom engaging him in a sexual act in the front seat while he was driving. I remember feeling very dirty and ashamed. While this was taking place, we stopped at a light and I saw my dad standing on the street corner next to us. Terrified, I ducked down behind the seat, hoping he wouldn't see us. Later that night we went to the other guy's house; my mom had sex with him while I lay outside the room.

When I was about seven, my mom married Alex, who was very abusive to her and to me. One night he beat her so bad that she had to be rushed away in an ambulance. Shortly after that, she packed up our stuff and ran to this other guy Miguel's apartment; Miguel was also a drug dealer.

At first Miguel was very nice to me, but it wasn't long before his true colors showed. He also became physically abusive with my mom. When my mom would leave to go to work, Miguel would make up inappropriate games that involved him touching me and me touching him. There was also a man named Julio who slept in the hallway of the apartment. I slept in the living room. In the morning when my mom was still passed out, I would be up by myself.

Julio also began to make up games. One time after one of these games there was semen all over my nightgown. I remember going in and sitting against the wall, feeling very dirty. I was very confused. I thought it was my fault for allowing it to happen—for not trying to stop it. I thought I did something to provoke it. I remember the cat coming over to me and rubbing his body against mine; I picked him up and threw him across the room. I then took off my nightgown and hid it so my mom wouldn't see it.

Around this time a friend invited me to church. I don't remember much except them singing the song "Jesus loves me" and that I could pray to Jesus when I was scared. I began to pray that my mom and dad would get back together and that I would have my own room. I didn't know my dad well but my brother seemed to be happy so I figured it had to be better than what I was going through.

Shortly after my church visit, my mother and I ended up leaving Miguel's place, the apartment where I had been sexually abused. We went and stayed at a cottage on the side of my grandpa's house. One evening my mother and I were sitting outside talking to her friend. I was sitting on the back of a truck with her friend and my mother was facing us with her back turned against the street. I saw the man who had molested me and abused my mom walking angrily behind my mom. I tried to warn her but no words would come out. I tried so hard but tears just welled up and I fell to the ground. The man came up behind her and punched her.

All I remember next was running across the street to the hotel. When I ran into the hotel, they could see something was very wrong by the terror on my face. I tried to speak but still nothing would come out. I don't know what happened next except that cops were there. The next thing I remember was being in the apartment

> ⍟ ⍟
>
> Around this time a friend invited me to church. I don't remember much except them singing the song "Jesus loves me" and that I could pray to Jesus when I was scared.
>
> Elizabeth
>
> ⍟ ⍟

64

begging my mom not to leave me but she did. She left me with her friend (the man she had been outside talking to).

That night she ended up hitting someone with her car while she was drunk. The cops brought her back to the house; I guess to check on me. I remember them trying to wake me up, and I was trying to wake up but it was like I was drugged. I think it was because my body had just gone through such shock and trauma… The next morning I woke up and the guy was sleeping on the couch. I wasn't sure if it had been a dream or not but my mom wasn't there. So I put on my shoes and left to find my mom.

I began to walk; I knew if I went straight that would take me toward the beach where I just had to go left and then that would lead me to where I thought my mom was. That's where Miguel, the man who molested me, lived; I thought my mom would be there. After walking for awhile I decided to turn around. When I arrived back at the cottage my mom's girlfriend was there to pick me up. She said that I just missed HRS who was there to take me into custody.

My mother ended up going to jail and rehab for a year. I stayed with my mom's girlfriend for awhile. It was a little weird because my mom had been sleeping with her husband. One time I was sleeping on the floor and they were having sex and I got up and turned the light on hoping that it would make them stop but it didn't. They just kicked me out on the couch and continued making loud noises. During my stay at their house, their older daughter began to molest me. After awhile my father came for me and took me to live with him.

After my mom got out of jail, my mom and dad remarried; I eventually got my own room. I knew God had answered my prayers. I always sensed God was there and would often pray. Things were better although my mom did start drinking again but at least my dad never hit her. My father drank also but he was a hard worker and always made sure the bills were paid. He came across as cold and unaffectionate; that felt like a good thing considering where I had been.

When I was about 9 or 10, I spent the night at my friend's house and her father showed us pornography and looked at our breasts, telling us what kind of breasts we were going to have. I don't remember what happened after or before.

As I grew up I became a product of my environment. At the age of twelve, I went to the house of a boy I liked. I thought we would just hang out and maybe kiss, but he had something else in mind. He ended up putting a pillow over my head and taking my virginity. I was paralyzed by fear. It was a long, shameful walk home. I cried for a very long time. After that incident I began using drugs. I masked my pain with anger and drugs. And I didn't trust anyone.

I learned at a very young age to keep secrets. I lived with a lot of anxiety and fear. I began to cut myself to relive my pain. My self-hatred grew very intense and continued down a very destructive path. I had no respect for myself or anyone else. At sixteen I had been with my brother and some friends getting high. I blacked out and the next thing I remember was waking up in my brother's friend's bed with him on top of me. After that happened, I felt betrayed; it validated my feelings of low self-worth. I felt that it was my fault for being in that situation, so I kept it a secret. I lost it after that and went on a long drug binge. Not knowing I was pregnant, I continued to use drugs until I had a miscarriage.

During this time my step-grandfather (who was an alcoholic) was living with us. He

ဆ သ

After my mom got out of jail, my mom and dad remarried; I eventually got my own room. I knew God had answered my prayers. I always sensed God was there and would often pray.

Elizabeth

ဆ သ

would give me rides to work and give me money. He began to hug me inappropriately and sneakily rub his hand against my breast. My mom was constantly getting drunk and trying to kill herself. I was always either running away or getting kicked out.

I ended up going to a shelter when I was sixteen. I was at the shelter on and off until I was eighteen. I did the drug program there a couple times. I worked a few jobs and eventually had enough money to get my own place. After leaving the shelter I continued to do drugs but this time I was a functioning addict. Long story short: I ended up getting pregnant and having a healthy baby girl.

Through some very traumatic trials and tribulations I came to know the Lord Jesus Christ. In a nut shell, my father ended up dying unexpectedly at the age of 49 from a drug overdose, my mother went to a psych ward and my brother got sentenced to ten years for DUI manslaughter.

The Lord knew what it would take for me to surrender completely. The Lord bought an amazing pastor and his wife into my life who took me and my daughter into their home and mentored me.

When I first got saved, so much trauma had taken place that the Lord had to help me through that first. However, after being saved a few years, I couldn't understand why I was still struggling with depression, anger and thoughts of suicide. I would go for counseling and they would tell me I just need to spend more time in the word and pray. This only made me more frustrated so I stopped going to counseling and tried to deal with it on my own.

After some time the Lord began to reveal to me through other people and His word that there were some deep-rooted issues that had been swept under the rug and needed to be addressed. I've been on my healing journey now for a couple years. I've realized through counseling that my self-destructive thought patterns started at a very young age. I realized I had to start changing the way I viewed myself and start seeing myself as a new creation. I struggled for a long time with the whole "new creation thing" because of how I felt about myself and the un-forgiveness I had towards myself. I think I blamed myself more than anyone for the abuse that had taken place and for not being able to protect my mom.

That was one of the first lies I recognized, discovering it wasn't my job to protect my mom. It was her job to protect me. The other lie was that I'm unlovable and unclean. I never blamed God for what happened to me because I knew that we live in a fallen world. But there was a point during this healing process that I wept for the innocence and purity I lost at such young age.

I was angry towards the Lord because I felt like I was never given a chance. There was always something there from a young age to make me feel dirty and I realized I never knew what it truly was to feel clean. That night while I was weeping I opened up my Bible and it took me to Psalm 103:2-5 *"Praise the Lord, O my soul and forget not all His benefits—who forgives all your sins and heals all your diseases, who redeems your life from the pit and crowns you with love and compassion, who satisfies your desires with good things so that your youth is renewed like the eagle's."*

The Lord also reminded me that night about Luke 7:47 where Jesus says about the prostitute, *"I tell you, her many sins have been forgiven—for she loved much. But he who has been forgiven of little loves little."* I felt the Lord spoke to my spirit that night that I need to view myself and the pain that I have endured as a precious jewel and that He loves me unconditionally and I need to learn to love myself unconditionally and believe that I'm indeed a new beloved creation of His. Regardless of how man may judge me I need to stand firm in my new identity in Christ.

The other lie that I recognized was that I would magically be healed from all my baggage. I don't get depressed and angry like I used to. I've realized what my red flags are. For example when I start to feel depressed I don't isolate anymore. Instead I seek counsel and try to journal which is very helpful in my helping me process my feelings and deciphering the truth from the lies.

I also am careful with the company I keep and make sure that they are people who are encouraging and who will point me back to the Lord. I'm still working on forgiveness with my mom. She has been in a drug program for the last eight months and I do see her a couple times a month. I have told her I forgive her; however, when there are new flashbacks that come up, I have to continue to forgive her.

I realize that this is going to be a process but I know that there is a freedom and a liberty that comes when I choose to forgive. When I read the story about Joseph that really ministered to me because of how he was able to forgive his brothers for selling into him into slavery and how he was able to forgive Potiphar who threw him into prison. Joseph said in Genesis 50:20, *"You intended to harm but God intended it for good, to accomplish what is now being done, the saving of many lives"* (NIV). I found this to be true in my own life. What the enemy did to destroy me, God is using to bring others to Himself through my testimony of hope. I no longer view myself as victim but instead I view myself as a victor and new vibrant confident woman in Christ.

As you read Elizabeth's story, what emotions did you experience? _____

_____

_____

_____

_____

In what ways do you identify with her experiences? _____

_____

_____

_____

_____

_____

Perhaps you, like Elizabeth, have tried cutting yourself to release your pain. The book "Inside a Cutter's Mind," by Jerusha Clark with Dr. Earl Henslin (NavPress) can help you understand self-harm and discover alternatives for releasing your pain.

The Lord is my rock, my fortress, and my savior; my God is my rock, in whom I find protection. He is my shield, the power that saves me, and my place of safety. I called on the Lord, who is worthy of praise, and he saved me from my enemies.

Psalm 18:2-3, NLT

---

3. Day Three: **Forgiveness Doesn't Necessarily Include Reconciliation**

After reading Elizabeth's story, it's obvious that it wouldn't be safe for her to contact the drug dealers and others who molested her throughout her childhood. Though Elizabeth forgave her mom and reconciled with her, she is consistently protective of her own daughter. Due to her mom's ongoing struggle with drug use, Elizabeth knows it would not be safe to leave her little girl in her grandma's care.

People who insist that forgiveness includes "reunion" do not understand that tangible consequences of molestation for the perpetrator include the survivor's right to be safe from further emotional, physical, spiritual or mental harm. Being safe may prevent you being with those who committed the crime of sexual abuse, even if they are close family members. Forgiving your offender does not remove legal or relational consequences of the offense.

Many survivors of sexual abuse have been told they are being "unchristian" if they won't fully reconcile with their perpetrator because "the Bible says to 'forget what lies behind.'" Not only could that sort of reasoning expose an individual to more abuse; it misrepresents what the apostle Paul wrote in Philippians 3:10-14 (NIV).

 Explore - *I want to know Christ and the power of his resurrection and the fellowship of sharing in his sufferings, becoming like him in his death, and so, somehow, to attain to the resurrection from the dead. Not that I have already obtained all this, or have already been made perfect, but I press on to take hold of that for which Christ Jesus took hold of me. Brothers, I do not consider myself yet to have taken hold of it. But one thing I do: Forgetting what is behind and straining toward what is ahead, I press on toward the goal to win the prize for which God has called me heavenward in Christ Jesus.*

Using the language of athletic competition, Paul does urge us to forget what lies behind. However, in Philippians 3, he is not talking about erasing the past and its irreparable challenges. He is not ordering you to reunite with someone whose damaging behaviors could cause you to be wounded again and again.

Instead, God offers a healing gift: the opportunity to continually move forward into the wonderful freedom and intimacy He offers you forever, through Christ. As you realize you can learn to trust, you can make the choice to move into the healing relationship God offers. You can discover that knowing Him is so wonderful it is worth giving up anything that hinders recognizing who He really is. God's amazing gift for you includes new life now and new hope for a future of safe, kind, and loving fellowship with God in your daily life.

⚭ ⚮

Forgiveness is an act of the will, and the will can function regardless of the temperature of the heart.[50]

Corrie Ten Boom

⚭ ⚮

In what ways can you begin to make the choice to "give up" past hurts and discover deeper intimacy with God? _____

_____

_____

_____

_____

_____

_____

Accepting new life from God and actually beginning to live it will involve new activities, new choices, new goals and new hope. Look for ideas in your local newspaper, church newsletter, gym, book club, online events' listing, or community calendar. List several activities that could help you expand your horizons: _____

_____

_____

_____

_____

Even when you decide to "press on toward the goal," you can feel emotional pain. Pause and read Psalms 42, 43, and 71, looking for a repeated theme of discouragement transformed by God to hope. What themes did you notice?

_____

_____

_____

_____

_____

Why are you cast down, O my inner self? And why should you moan over me and be disquieted within me? Hope in God and wait expectantly for Him, for I shall yet praise Him, Who is the help of my countenance, and my God. Psalm 42:11, AMP

The Bible doesn't avoid real concerns. God knows your perpetrator's evil choices can cause you to feel ashamed, worthless and alone. He wants you to fully comprehend that your life matters—and that you have mattered to Him since before you were born.

For You are my hope; O Lord God, You are my trust from my youth and the source of my confidence. Upon You have I leaned and relied from birth; You are He Who took me from my mother's womb and You have been my benefactor from that day. My praise is continually of You. I am as a wonder and surprise to many, but You are my strong refuge.

Psalm 71:5-7, AMP

ജ ര

In your hands you hold the seeds of failure or the potential for greatness. Your hands are capable, but they must be used and for the right things to reap the rewards you are capable of attaining. The choice is yours.[51]

Zig Ziglar

ജ ര

69

When you feel discouraged, you don't have to either *give up or give in* to dejection or despair. After thinking about Philippians 3 and Psalms 42, 43 and 71, what can you do to move from discouragement to authentic hope? Use the space provided to list what causes you to be discouraged and what you can do to experience hope.

Causes of Discouragement	To experience hope, I can...

God says He is a _____ when you are oppressed, a refuge in times of trouble (see Psalm 9:8-9). "Oppressed" can also mean tyrannized, coerced, or burdened. Think about how God offers you refuge—a safe haven—and journal about finding protection from your past in Him: *He will judge the world with justice and rule the nations with fairness. The Lord is a shelter for the oppressed, a refuge in times of trouble* (Psalm 9:8-9, NLT).

_____
_____
_____
_____
_____
_____
_____
_____

In Psalm 9:8-9, what does God promise to do about injustice? _____
_____
_____
_____

The prophet Jeremiah, often referred to as "the weeping prophet," described God's promise to exiled Israel.

 Explore - *For I know the thoughts and plans that I have for you, says the Lord, thoughts and plans for welfare and peace and not for evil, to give you hope in your final outcome. Then you will call upon Me, and you will come and pray to Me, and I will hear and heed you.*

Jeremiah 29:11-12, AMP

You, too, might feel like an exile or outcast. You might feel discouraged about lost years, vanished dreams. Please pause and consider: your past does not need to define your future.

Read Jeremiah 29:11-12 again, considering that you matter to God. Realize He wants to give you a future of hope, peace and safety—then respond to the following statements, allowing yourself to hope:

When God thinks about me, He _____
_____
_____
_____

Since His plans for me include a future and hope, I will _____
_____
_____
_____

After thinking about the challenges inherent in "forgetting," what do you think about the choice to forgive? _____
_____
_____
_____
_____

ജ ന

O Lord, I give my life to you. I trust in you, my God! Do not let me be disgraced, or let my enemies rejoice in my defeat. No one who trusts in you will ever be disgraced, but disgrace comes to those who try to deceive others.

Psalm 25:1-3, NLT

ജ ന

4. Day Four: **Forgiveness, Safety and Justice**

Some family members who told you not to discuss your abuse might have been molested themselves and never dealt with their own abuse. Others are in dysfunctional relationships and would rather protect the perpetrator than their own child. Some mothers fear being beaten or rejected by boyfriends who molest their children. That is not an excuse; it is NEVER OK for an adult to allow a child to be molested.

When a daughter comes home, bloodied with torn clothing, she needs help; she needs comfort. Instead of providing help, some parents actually order their daughter to "Never tell anyone about this!" That adds rejection, fear, blame and further trauma to the horror she already feels. If you have been raped, TELL someone who can help! Go to a hospital; get a physical examination. Report the crime to the police so you can get the help you need, whether anyone encourages you to do so or not.

An adult—whether a parent, youth worker, teacher, pastor, neighbor or friend—who knows about or suspects someone is being molested should report it IMMEDIATELY to local police or the toll-free abuse hotline (800.96ABUSE - 800.962.2873). Calls can be made anonymously, so don't let fear of repercussions excuse you from your responsibility to report.

Has your family been supportive of your healing journey? ___Yes ___ No

If you answered "No," journal about how you will include them in your forgiveness process. _____

_____

_____

_____

_____

_____

_____

_____

_____

_____

_____

_____

_____

_____

&0 C&

An adult— whether a parent, youth worker, teacher, pastor, neighbor or friend—who knows about or suspects someone is being molested should report it IMMEDIATELY to local police or the toll-free abuse hotline.

800.96ABUSE
800.962.2873

&0 C&

1984 Nobel Peace Prize winner Archbishop Desmond Tutu is known for his successful struggle as an anti-apartheid activist in his native South Africa. He said, "If you are neutral in situations of injustice, you have chosen the side of the oppressor. If an elephant has its foot on the tail of a mouse and you say that you are neutral, the mouse will not appreciate your neutrality."[52]

In regard to forgiveness, Desmond Tutu stated, "Forgiving is not forgetting; it's actually remembering—remembering and not using your right to hit back. It's a second chance for a new beginning. And the remembering part is particularly important. Especially if you don't want to repeat what happened." [53]

As you consider both of Desmond Tutu's statements, the first about neutrality in the face of injustice and the second about forgiving but not forgetting, journal below about how you can apply these ideas to your situation: _____

_____

_____

_____

_____

_____

_____

_____

_____

_____

_____

Many people resist forgiveness because they think it will take the offender "off the hook," fearing justice will never occur if they forgive. In a real sense, though, forgiveness is taking the offender off your "hook" and putting him or her on God's "hook."

Read the following verses. In the space below, write down your observations about your understanding of God's attitude toward justice.

The Lord loves righteousness and justice; the earth is full of his unfailing love. Psalm 33:5, NIV

O Lord, you hear the desire of the afflicted; you will strengthen their heart; you will incline your ear to do justice to the fatherless and the oppressed, so that man who is of the earth may strike terror no more. Psalm 10:17-18, ESV

_____

_____

_____

_____

_____

_____

_____

_____

_____

_____

ℰ☯ ℭ℠

Many people resist forgiveness because they think it will take the offender "off the hook," fearing justice will never occur if they forgive. In a real sense, though, forgiveness is taking the offender off your "hook" and putting him or her on God's "hook."

ℰ☯ ℭ℠

5. Day Five: **My Forgiveness Journey**

Today and this weekend, review chapter six, considering new insights you've gained or questions you still have about forgiving. Whether your offender was a family member, friend, teacher, or stranger, forgiveness is something you do without ever being "forced" to get in contact with that person.

In Luke, Jesus explained one important aspect of forgiveness: *Jesus said, "This is how you should pray: "Father, may your name be kept holy. May your Kingdom come soon. Give us each day the food we need, and forgive us our sins, as we forgive those who sin against us. And don't let us yield to temptation"* (Luke 11:2-4, NLT).

A second reason for forgiveness follows the first. Forgiveness protects us from carrying around rotting bitterness that festers in our souls long after someone wounds us. Those raw soul-wounds can fuel sullen resentment deep within your soul, defining everything you do, even when you aren't aware of it. Those who won't forgive can be easily triggered to feelings of anger, frustration, irritation, jealousy or hurt. They can feel like victims in any situation. Or they can feel compelled to "rescue" anyone who is hurting, seldom stopping to wonder why they are continually exhausted from endlessly caring for others' needs.

Choosing to forgive is not choosing to forget. After you make the choice to forgive, each time you remember the offense, you can tell yourself, "I distinctly remember forgiving that." When you do that, the emotional pain of your abuse will gradually fade as you allow yourself to live in the new emotions God provides.

A misunderstanding of forgiveness can expose others to harm similar to what you experienced. If you are a parent, it is your responsibility to be sure your own children are never alone in the presence of your molester. If your child's grandparent, aunt, uncle or other relative is the one who molested you, do not allow your former molester to babysit, even when your child or children are asleep. Only supervised visits, with your child always within your sight, are safe, and perhaps even those are not safe. Each situation varies; it is a parent's job to understand the situation and protect her children so another generation does not experience the anguish of sexual molestation.

Understanding forgiveness helps us realize that reconciliation is not always possible. There are times when forgiveness leads to reconciliation, but that would only be after the survivor of sexual abuse knows she and others can be 100% safe. It would also require that the offender demonstrate long-term repentance, with years of tangible evidence of total change from past behavior. [However, since sexual abuse can occur rapidly, in secret, it is not a good idea to blithely accept an offender's promises of changed behavior or to entrust one's children, for even a limited amount of time,

૪૦ ૦૪

Forgiving is the only way to heal the wounds of a past we cannot change and cannot forget. Forgiving changes a bitter memory into a grateful memory, a cowardly memory into a courageous memory, an enslaved memory into a free memory. Forgiving restores a self-respect that someone killed.[54]

Lewis B. Smedes

૪૦ ૦૪

alone with a "repentant" sex offender. That is simply not a wise idea, no matter what you are told.] Reconciliation requires a restoration of trust,which is rarely possible due to the extensive core damage of sexual molestation.

When you forgive, you are not condoning what your perpetrator did; you are not saying those who didn't protect you did nothing wrong. You cannot look on your abuse as unimportant or inconsequential.

Forgiveness understands the abuse is so serious and so damaging that choosing not to forgive will give the abuse power over the rest of your life. Instead of holding on to other people's offenses, you can entrust yourself to God's perfect care.

How you will apply your insights about forgiveness in your daily life?

_____
_____
_____
_____
_____

Are you safe being in contact with the one(s) who molested you? _____

_____
_____
_____
_____

It is not selfish to be safe. As you recognize your need to be safe, are you experiencing resistance from others? _____

_____
_____
_____
_____
_____

What will you do to keep growing and learning, even when facing opposition? _____

_____
_____
_____
_____

Because forgiveness is such an essential aspect of your healing journey, the next chapter will continue to explore this important theme.

∞ ∞

Relax in My [Jesus] healing, holy Presence. Be still, while I transform your heart and mind. Let go of cares and worries, so that you can receive My Peace.[55]

Sarah Young

∞ ∞

Forgive and Go Forward

Chapter Seven

One day as Peter was discussing forgiveness with Jesus, he asked Jesus how many times he had to forgive when his brother sinned against him. Thinking he was being very noble, Peter asked, "Up to seven times?" Peter's suggestion was generous, because traditional rabbinic teaching told an offended person to forgive a brother only three times. But Jesus responded that forgiveness needs to be exercised much more; not seven times, but "seventy times seven," or 490 times. What Jesus was expressing was that no limits should be set on how many times we forgive (Bible Knowledge Commentary, Matthew 18:21-22).

Forgiveness is difficult, and it is a process. According to Lewis B. Smedes, "The question is never how many times we are *supposed* to forgive, but how many times we *need* to forgive. Forgiving is a gift, not a duty. It is meant to heal, not to obligate."[56]

Core Healing Goal: to understand and apply three steps of forgiveness.

1. Day One: **Remembering to Forgive**

   Forgiveness enables you to accept God's provision of a new way of living. Choosing to forgive can release you from the trauma of past abuse and provide new opportunities for healing and growth for the rest of your life. One obstacle to forgiveness, though, is the incorrect belief that one has to remember everything that happened before making the choice to forgive.

   Just as people with severe physical injuries often are unable to remember significant details of car accidents or other physical trauma, so people who have experienced the physical, emotional, mental and spiritual trauma of sexual abuse often cannot remember specific details of what happened.

   Be careful you don't "force yourself" to remember. Some people have wrongly severed ties with family members after a well-meaning but untrained counselor led them to remember "false memories," influencing them to "discover" fictional depictions of abuse that never happened. For months or years, a person introduced to false memories could wrongly believe in the occurrence of nonexistent events, resulting in needless complications and profound sorrow for themselves and those they falsely accuse.

   Pause for a moment, simply allowing yourself to relax in the confidence that your healing journey does not demand you push yourself to remember every traumatic detail, then write about what you are experiencing _____

   _____

   _____

   _____

Forgiving is a personal experience that happens inside one person at a time. What happens to the other person, the one we forgive, is up to him.[57]

Lewis B. Smedes

It may be impossible to recall everything about your sexual abuse, especially if it happened in early childhood. Another difficulty regarding trying to remember everything about your past is that the process of recalling aspects of past trauma could severely re-traumatize you. You could ask numerous people and get numerous accounts of what happened, leaving you more confused than when you began trying to discover what really happened.

For you to experience hope and healing, it is not necessary to remember every incident of your past or recall all incidents of abuse that happened to you. You can make the following verses from Psalm 139:23-24 (NASU) your prayer throughout your healing process:

Search me, O God, and know my heart; try me and know my anxious thoughts; and see if there be any hurtful way in me, and lead me in the everlasting way.

You can safely trust God to lead you to what you need to remember—and to keep you from what you do not need to recall. You can ask Him to help you recall repressed memories that need to be dealt with and to keep you protected from re-experiencing the trauma of events you can safely entrust to His care without revisiting those parts of your past.

As you pray Psalm 139:23-24, ask God to make you aware of specific people you need to forgive, including all who molested you and all those who could have protected you but did not.

People I need to forgive for molesting me: _____

_____

_____

_____

_____

_____

People I need to forgive who could have stopped the abuse but didn't: _____

_____

_____

_____

_____

_____

_____

If you have felt hurt by people who didn't understand your abuse, they could be added to your list as well. Then write each name (or the person's initials, or some other symbol that helps you remember who you're forgiving); use a separate page if you desire. As God leads, add other names to your list. (Keep these lists for the work we'll do later this week.)

> ৪০ ೮೮
>
> When we have been deeply and unjustly hurt, it is tempting to give in and be bitter. That is a battle that we cannot afford to lose. Center your attention on God.[58]
>
> Chris Brauns
>
> ৪০ ೮೮

2. Day Two: **Grudges, Resentment and Other Destructive Choices**

If you don't forgive, your abuse will continue to define you. Like a hamster running circles in a wheel all day, every day; choosing to remain in resentment keeps you going nowhere.

William H. Walton said, "To carry a grudge is like being stung to death by one bee." [59]

Are you carrying a grudge? _____ Explain _____

_____

_____

_____

How is carrying a grudge like "being stung to death by one bee"? _____

_____

_____

෨ ෬

As much as we might like forgiveness to be quick and easy, it is a process. [60]

Dr. David Stoop
Dr. James Masteller

෨ ෬

To understand the destructive power of resentment, grudges and bitterness, consider the story of a sheriff in a small Midwestern town. Very little happened in that town, even on Main Street, where there was a small bank, a tiny grocery store, a bar and the sheriff's office. The only crimes in that community took place on rare occasions when a drunk got obnoxious or a teenager drove too fast during the weekend. The sheriff had a jail cell in his office, but he never had prisoners in it. Instead, he used the cell for storing paper towels, coffee filters and the few other office supplies he kept on hand.

Imagine his surprise the day he actually captured a criminal. Hearing a lot of commotion outside his office, he stepped outside and saw someone bolting out of the bank, gun in hand. The sheriff surprised the robber—and himself—by rushing to the scene and arresting him.

He grudgingly moved office supplies out of the jail cell to make room for his prisoner, "Billy Bob." As soon as he locked Billy Bob up, the sheriff called the county jail to let them know he'd be bringing Billy Bob to their facility, only twenty miles away. He was horrified to find out the county jail was full. "Well, when can I bring him in?" he asked the clerk impatiently. "Not for awhile. We'll let you know in writing when we have space for your prisoner here," she told him.

At first, the sheriff was irritated by the inconvenience of having to share his cozy office with someone else. His irritation quickly turned to rage when he realized his prisoner was obnoxious! Billy Bob's body odor dominated the entire building; his language was foul; and he threw the food the sheriff brought him all over the cell, complaining constantly about the menu, the taste and the sheriff's "absolutely inhumane" treatment.

The sheriff hired someone to take his place at the jail three nights a week so he could go home to be with his family. He complained to his wife, "We can't even leave town to go on vacation; my whole world is dominated by this prisoner." He smelled his arm, groaning, "I think I'm even starting to smell like him!"

When the county called him a few weeks later to say they had a cell available, what do you think the sheriff did? He handcuffed Billy Bob and drove him immediately to the county jail. The bank robber would still have to pay for his crime; the sheriff was simply giving up his responsibility to bring a criminal to justice.

You can do what the sheriff did. He released Billy Bob—and all the horrible things about him, including his destructive behavior—to a higher authority. Billy Bob's criminal behavior was not being ignored. Releasing your perpetrator liberates you from what happened; it doesn't liberate your perpetrator.

Do you want to take your abuser with you everywhere you go for the rest of your life? ____ Yes ____ No

As you consider the sheriff's choice to release a criminal to serve his sentence elsewhere, how do you think it felt not to have to listen to, smell, or deal with Billy Bob every day? _____
_____
_____
_____

You don't have to "feel like" releasing your offender to do so. How might you feel when you choose to release your offender(s) to God? _____
_____
_____
_____

Journal your response about how you will entrust your abuser to God, the author of justice. _____
_____
_____
_____
_____
_____
_____
_____

છ૭ ૭ઝ

...forgiving is the only way to get ourselves free from the trap of persistent and unfair pain. Far from being unfair, it is the only way for a victim to be fair to himself or herself. Far from being a dishonest denial of reality, forgiving is not even possible unless we own the painful truth of what happened to us.[61]

Lewis B. Smedes

છ૭ ૭ઝ

3. Day Three: **How to Forgive**

In chapter six, Elizabeth mentioned that the story of Joseph's life helped her understand forgiveness. Joseph provides rich examples of someone who could have easily become bitter; instead, he made intentional choices to forgive each time he experienced the anguish of betrayal, abandonment, unfair treatment or cruelty.

Please take a few moments to read and consider Genesis chapters 37 through 39, noticing some of the events that affected Joseph's life. His mother died giving birth to his younger brother, leaving him with ten stepbrothers and his infant brother. All ten of his stepbrothers resented him because he was their father's favorite. Some of Joseph's brothers wanted to kill him and lie to their father about what happened. After discussion, most of the stepbrothers agreed to sell him into slavery instead.

Joseph's brothers accepted payment from Ishmaelite traders and watched their brother be taken away as a slave. Then they dipped his tunic in goat's blood and took it to their father, who recognized his favorite son's special tunic and concluded "a wild beast has devoured him. Without doubt Joseph is torn to pieces" (Genesis 37:33, NKJV). Even though they watched their father suffer prolonged grief, the brothers did not confess their lie—or their actions.

What did you notice in Genesis 37-39 that relates to you? _____

_____
_____
_____
_____
_____
_____
_____
_____
_____
_____
_____
_____
_____
_____
_____
_____
_____
_____

80 80

Forgiveness is not an occasional act; it is a permanent attitude.[62]

Martin Luther King, Jr.

80 80

Taken by slave traders to a foreign land with no way to contact his father, Joseph landed a "great job" as a slave and was actually doing well. Then disaster occurred again: he was falsely accused and unfairly imprisoned (see Genesis 39:1-20). Forgotten in prison, he didn't become bitter. Instead, Joseph was such a positive influence that the prison warden *"put Joseph in charge of all those held in the prison, and he was made responsible for all that was done there"* (Genesis 39:22).

The amazing story continues when Joseph is released from prison to become Prime Minister of Egypt, second-in-charge to Pharaoh (keep reading Genesis chapters 40 and 41 to discover that astonishing series of events).

The God of the Old Testament is the same God of the New Testament. The Bible promises, *"And we know that God causes all things to work together for good to those who love God, to those who are called according to His purpose"* (Romans 8:28, NASU).

Think of your life at this point in time. Will you entrust your current sorrows and concerns to God, accepting His gracious provision of new hope, new life, and a new beginning? Write out your response as a prayer to God:

_____

_____

_____

_____

_____

_____

_____

_____

_____

_____

_____

_____

_____

_____

> ⬧ ⬧
>
> It is freeing to become aware that we do not have to be victims of our past and can learn new ways of responding. But there is a step beyond this recognition... it is the step of forgiveness. Forgiveness is love practiced among people who love poorly. It sets us free without wanting anything in return.[63]
>
> Henri Nouwen
>
> ⬧ ⬧

Joseph was used by God to keep Egypt from death by famine, because he trusted God amidst repeated heartbreak. Joseph's ten stepbrothers, in danger of starvation in their own land, traveled to Egypt to purchase grain for their families' survival. They had no idea they were entrusting their survival to the brother they betrayed. You can read this compelling story in Genesis chapters 42 through 46. One result of Joseph's faithfulness was that his entire family was saved from starvation and moved to Egypt where there was still food.

When Joseph's father died after their people's move to Egypt, his brothers were sure Joseph would demand revenge for their hideous betrayal years ago, despite the fact that he had faithfully taken care of them for years. Genesis 50:15-21 (NIV) describes what happened:

 Explore - *When Joseph's brothers saw that their father was dead, they said, 'What if Joseph holds a grudge against us and pays us back for all the wrongs we did to him?' So they sent word to Joseph, saying, "Your father left these instructions before he died: 'This is what you are to say to Joseph: I ask you to forgive your brothers the sins and the wrongs they committed in treating you so badly.' Now please forgive the sins of the servants of the God of your father.' When their message came to him, Joseph wept. His brothers then came and threw themselves down before him. 'We are your slaves,' they said. But Joseph said to them, 'Don't be afraid. Am I in the place of God? You intended to harm me, but God intended it for good to accomplish what is now being done, the saving of many lives. So then, don't be afraid. I will provide for you and your children.' And he reassured them and spoke kindly to them.*

The Latin counterpart of the English verb "to forgive" is "condono" or "condonare," meaning "to give away; present." Joseph gave away his right to demand his brothers pay for their crime of selling him (who they did not own) into slavery, forcing him away from everything and everyone he had known and loved. Instead, Joseph chose to entrust himself to God and rely on Him to provide justice in His way and in His time.

It is important to distinguish the difference between what happened to Joseph and what happened to you. There is no sense that what happened to you was OK or that it served some positive purpose in your family system. There is nothing "positive" about sexual abuse! As we discussed in chapter six, an important aspect of forgiveness is that it does not necessarily involve further contact with your abuser. There are many situations in which it would not be safe to have renewed contact with the person or persons who molested you.

If you do confront your abuser, he might deny what happened, showing no remorse. He might even blame you! You do not have to accept your abuser's denial or his blame. If you confront those who didn't protect you, they might excuse their own or the perpetrator's behavior.

Prayerfully consider your safety throughout each step of this process. **For your spiritual, emotional, mental and physical safety, it often is better to quietly forgive, in obedience to God, without confronting your perpetrator. God can perfectly accomplish direct confrontation without human help.**

ℬ ℭ

It is important to distinguish the difference between what happened to Joseph and what happened to you. There is no sense that what happened to you was OK or that it served some positive purpose in your family system. There is nothing "positive" about sexual abuse!

ℬ ℭ

What positive lessons about forgiveness do you notice in Joseph's story?

_____

_____

_____

How can you apply those lessons to your concerns? _____

_____

_____

_____

After considering the Latin meaning of "to forgive," translated from "condono" or "condonare," meaning "to give away; present," will you give away everything you hold against each person who wounded you?

_____ Yes _____ No   Why? _____

_____

Will you entrust your suffering to God, expecting His justice, healing and hope? _____ Yes _____ No   Why? _____

_____

_____

_____

All the evil things done to you have no power to define the rest of your life, unless you choose to hold onto past wounds. If you will not "give away" others' offenses to God, those hurts and sorrows will continue to exert power over your life.

When you choose to forgive, God releases you from being dominated by others' sins. *"For sin shall not [any longer] exert dominion over you, since now you are not under Law [as slaves], but under grace [as subjects of God's favor and mercy]."* Romans 6:14, AMP

If you choose to confront your perpetrator directly as part of the forgiveness process, seek wise advice before you prayerfully proceed. Remember, "...in the multitude of counselors there is safety" (Proverbs 11:14b, NKJV).

Journal about specific ways you will choose to live in God's grace today:

_____

_____

_____

_____

_____

_____

&ℭ &ℭ

Forgiveness unleashes joy. It brings peace. It washes the slate clean. It sets all the highest values of love in motion. In a sense, forgiveness is Christianity at its highest level.[64]

John MacArthur

&ℭ &ℭ

4. Day Four: **A New Perspective**

The good news about forgiveness is that **you can** experience it. You can make the choice to move forward with the clear realization that you have completed the process of recognizing the abuse and releasing your offender from your "hook" to God's "hook." Rather than minimizing the scope of damage inherent in sexual abuse, you have faced it. Now it's vital to know how to go forward, being released—freed—from past trauma.

Let's travel to Italy to continue understanding what forgiveness involves. In an important sense, forgiveness involves the choice to disentangle, or **untie**, yourself from the past. The Italian word for "untie" is "sciogliere." The etymology of this word comes from the Latin "solution," which means to "absolve one from debt." In the Latin-Italian dictionary "solutio" means "to loosen, to liberate or to resolve." The English translation is "sŏlūtĭo," which means "a loosing, unloosing, dissolution." Synonyms for "dissolution" include "termination," or "conclusion." This section will help you break free from the trauma of your past, untying yourself from the strangleholds of bitterness, rage, contempt, and revenge.

You could spend the rest of your life trying to determine **why** your abuse happened—and be stuck in a quagmire of unanswered questions. Asking **"Why?"** usually results in more questions than answers. Asking **"What?"** in an attempt to determine your perpetrators' motives or what really happened may leave you with a sense of futility; it is impossible to understand that depth of evil. Do not let your life be defined by someone who is living in defiance of God.

The question that can help you find workable answers now is **"How?"** In other words, you can look expectantly to your future instead of being defined by your past.

How will you choose to live today so that you are no longer defined by your abuse? _____

_____

_____

_____

_____

_____

_____

_____

Based on understanding God's provision of forgiveness, you can choose to forgive before you "feel like" forgiving. In fact, if you wait until you "feel ready" to forgive, you might never make the choice to act.

ဆ ၛ

Forgiveness is a redemptive response to having been wronged and wounded. This is simple but important.[65]

Lewis B. Smedes

ဆ ၛ

Do we forgive because of something God did, something we do, or because someone somehow "deserves" forgiveness? _____

_____

_____

Even though current events can trigger your memories of past trauma, your choice to forgive can stop the process of repeated emotional trauma. In the future, whenever you recall the abuse, you can recall God's provision of forgiveness instead of being agitated by the abuse over and over again. How can you apply this principle to your situation? _____

_____

_____

Since most acts of sexual abuse are committed by people known by the victim rather than by strangers, having continued contact with your perpetrator(s) presents complex challenges. As discussed in chapter six, many people think they have to reconcile with perpetrators who are family members. Consider what Scripture teaches about this:

Repay no one evil for evil. Have regard for good things in the sight of all men. If it is possible, as much as depends on you, live peaceably with all men. Beloved, do not avenge yourselves, but rather give place to wrath; for it is written, "Vengeance is Mine, I will repay," says the Lord. Romans 12:17-20, NKJV

Did you notice the phrase, "If it is possible..."? The passage continues, "...as much as depends on you, live peaceably with all men." It is not always possible to be at peace with everyone. However, even when it is impossible to reconcile with your abuser, you need to leave vengeance entirely in God's hands. He promises to deal with their offenses (see Romans 12:19).

 Explore - Jesus expressed God's viewpoint about sins against children: *He called a little child and had him stand among them. And he said: "I tell you the truth, unless you change and become like little children, you will never enter the kingdom of heaven. Therefore, whoever humbles himself like this child is the greatest in the kingdom of heaven. And whoever welcomes a little child like this in my name welcomes me. But if anyone causes one of these little ones who believe in me to sin, it would be better for him to have a large millstone hung around his neck and to be drowned in the depths of the sea."* Matthew 18:2-6 (NIV)

How did Jesus respond to children being mistreated? _____

_____

_____

ⅎ ⅏

Do we forgive because of something God did, something we do, or because someone somehow "deserves" forgiveness?

ⅎ ⅏

Jesus condemns actions that hurt children and erode their ability to trust. You can safely entrust your pain to Him, not only because He understands what you experienced but also because you matter to Him.

Forgiveness releases you from past trauma. As mentioned in chapter six, each time you feel anguish about what your abuser did or remember troubling details about the abuse, you can say "I distinctly remember forgiving that" so that others' evil choices do not identify the rest of your life. After you consciously choose to forgive—and keep reminding yourself you have done so, the emotional after-shocks of abuse will continue to diminish and fade away.

As you begin to comprehend your Savior's suffering, the intensity of your pain will diminish, overcome by His love.

 Explore - *This is the kind of life you've been invited into, the kind of life Christ lived. He suffered everything that came his way so you would know that it could be done, and also know how to do it, step-by-step. He never did one thing wrong, not once said anything amiss. They called him every name in the book and he said nothing back. He suffered in silence, content to let God set things right. He used his servant body to carry our sins to the Cross so we could be rid of sin, free to live the right way. His wounds became your healing. You were lost sheep with no idea who you were or where you were going. Now you're named and kept for good by the Shepherd of your souls* (1 Peter 2:21-25, THE MESSAGE).

How are you helped by considering Jesus' suffering, and the promise that "His wounds became your healing"? _____

_____

_____

_____

Confess to one another therefore your faults (your slips, your false steps, your offenses, your sins) and pray [also] for one another, that you may be healed and restored [to a spiritual tone of mind and heart]. The earnest (heartfelt, continued) prayer of a righteous man makes tremendous power available [dynamic in its working]. James 5:16, AMP

Pause and ask God if you need to ask anyone to forgive you for something you have done—or not done. Write down **what you need to do** and **when you will do it.** _____

_____

_____

_____

Do not let when you forgive depend on what someone else does (or does not do). What you can do instead is choose to **bless** those who abused you. (If you are reeling with shock after reading that statement, please keep reading!)

It is not 'forgive and forget' as if nothing wrong had ever happened, but 'forgive and go forward,' building on the mistakes of the past and the energy generated by reconciliation to create a new future.[66]

Carolyn Osiek

"Blessing" is not excusing. It is not tolerating wrong behavior or ignoring your suffering. Instead, it is recognizing that each of us answers to God for our own attitudes and actions.

Read the following verses, looking for three principles of forgiveness.

14 Bless those who persecute you; bless and do not curse.

17 Repay no one evil for evil. Have regard for good things in the sight of all men.

19 Beloved, do not avenge yourselves, but rather give place to wrath; for it is written, "Vengeance is Mine, I will repay," says the Lord.

Romans 12:14, 17,19, NKJV

Forgiveness Principle 1: _____

_____

Forgiveness Principle 2: _____

_____

Forgiveness Principle 3: _____

_____

When you bless your abuser, you aren't saying "Lord, give him a great life." You're not asking God to "Help her be happy today." What you are literally doing is entrusting every aspect of the situation to God, realizing He cannot bless evil.

Your choice to "bless" is an act of obedience to God. It is a practical step of forgiveness, releasing the burden of the other person's offenses fully to God. In this way, you free yourself from the painful emotions related to vengeance and entrust the challenging work to God. This is an intentional choice to quit trying to solve an unsolvable problem by yourself. As you relinquish control of your concerns to God, remember His promise to deal with evil.

Will you take the step to "bless"? Journal about your choice here: _____

_____

_____

_____

_____

_____

_____

_____

_____

_____

ℰℭ

Your choice to "bless" is an act of obedience to God. It is a practical step of forgiveness, releasing the burden of the other person's offenses fully to God.

ℰℭ

5. Day Five: **Writing, Releasing and Renewing**

To help you heal and grow, you can write forgiveness letters, reminding yourself you are doing this for your sake. The writing process is to help you forgive and go forward. When you finish writing your letters, you can shred them in a paper shredder or destroy them some other way, releasing all your concerns fully into God's unfailing love.

Writing forgiveness letters will help you remember your choice to forgive so that you can sincerely say, "I distinctly remember forgiving that," whenever painful memories are triggered in the future. You will then be able to quickly move forward, renewed in the awareness that you are free from your past trauma.

Write **today's date** here to help you remember your decision to forgive:

_____

Step One: Day One this week included making a list of everyone who wounded you. Please take time to prayerfully review your list, adding names as needed, asking God for wisdom as you begin writing. (Even if someone you need to forgive has died, you can still write that person a letter.)

Step Two: Remember the letters are designed to be a safe place for you to express the depth and significance of your hurt. **DO NOT MAIL your letters** unless you have someone helping you cope with potential new hurt.

Step Three: On separate pages, write a letter to each person on your list. As you write your letter(s), remember this activity is uniquely your own. The following are elements you can incorporate in your letter, choosing only what is helpful for your personal, private and original writing process.

- Describe what age(s) you were, your relationship to the abuser (or to the person who could have stopped the abuse but didn't) and the specific ways in which s/he hurt you (or allowed you to be hurt).

- Tell the perpetrator that she or he is fully responsible for the sexual abuse.

- Share what you thought and felt (e.g. "I thought I was trapped; I felt confused" or "numb" or "terrified," etc.) when it was happening.

- Write about what you have experienced since then.

- Share how you think and feel toward the perpetrator today.

- State how it should have been (example statements): "You were my stepdad; you should have protected me and loved me." - "You were my date; you pretended that you really cared for me. You lied when you said we were going to a movie and forced me into the back seat of your

> ❦ ❦
>
> ...I swore never to be silent whenever and wherever human beings endure suffering and humiliation. We must take sides. Neutrality helps the oppressor, never the victim. Silence encourages the tormentor, never the tormented.[67]
>
> Elie Wiesel
>
> ❦ ❦

car instead. You had no right to rob me of my virginity." - "You were my teacher. Teachers are supposed to keep kids safe, not trick them into doing oral sex in the closet." - "You are my aunt. An aunt should protect her nieces, not molest them and make them touch her."

- Explain that forgiveness does not necessarily include reconciliation; describe what kind of relationship, if any, you will have with the perpetrator in the future. State clear expectations and boundaries, including how you plan to keep yourself safe from further harm.

- Explain that the perpetrator needs to face consequences for the abuse. Forgiveness does not mean that the molester is being released from responsibility or even from potential legal consequences. Your forgiveness is not excusing others' harmful behavior.

- State what you are doing now to "untie" yourself from the abuser (e.g. "I am moving away from the stranglehold you've had on my mind, emotions and body. I am forgiving you so that I can be free from the evil you did to me").

As you write this letter, many emotions can surface. Pause to pray as you write, thinking about Psalm 139:23-24, allowing God to guide you in the writing process. Remember: the goal in writing forgiveness letters is being released from the past, not re-experiencing it. If the process of writing is more than you can bear, stop and review the previous chapters for encouragement and hope.

Renew your mind by listening to soothing music, reading a Psalm, or thanking God for the forgiveness He provides. Allow yourself to rest in His love, realizing you have moved from the trauma of your past into new hope for today—and for your future.

BE MERCIFUL and gracious to me, O God, be merciful and gracious to me, for my soul takes refuge and finds shelter and confidence in You; yes, in the shadow of Your wings will I take refuge and be confident until calamities and destructive storms are passed. I will cry to God Most High, Who performs on my behalf and rewards me [Who brings to pass His purposes for me and surely completes them]! He will send from heaven and save me from the slanders and reproaches of him who would trample me down or swallow me up, and He will put him to shame. Selah [pause, and calmly think of that]! God will send forth His mercy and loving-kindness and His truth and faithfulness. Psalm 57:1-3, AMP

HE WHO dwells in the secret place of the Most High shall remain stable and fixed under the shadow of the Almighty [Whose power no foe can withstand]. I will say of the Lord, He is my Refuge and my Fortress, my God; on Him I lean and rely, and in Him I [confidently] trust! For [then] He will deliver you from the snare of the fowler and from the deadly pestilence. [Then] He will cover you with His pinions, and under His wings shall you trust and find refuge; His truth and His faithfulness are a shield and a buckler. Psalm 91:1-4, AMP

Today and this weekend, review chapters six and seven, considering new insights you've gained or questions you still have about the choice to forgive. Allow yourself to simply relax in this moment, noticing God's compassion, becoming aware of His presence.

Journal what you are thinking and describe how you plan to apply what God has taught you about forgiveness.

_____
_____
_____
_____
_____
_____
_____
_____
_____
_____
_____
_____
_____
_____
_____
_____
_____
_____
_____
_____
_____
_____
_____
_____
_____
_____
_____
_____
_____

80 03

... memories aren't about *avoiding* responsibility; they're about *accepting* responsibility. They can help you determine what the deepest influences on you were so you can address your tendencies (some good, some bad) as a mature adult.[68]

Dr. Kevin Leman

80 03

Who Am I?

Take a few minutes to think about and write down your initial response to the question "Who Am I?"

_____

_____

_____

_____

_____

_____

_____

_____

_____

_____

_____

Review your responses, then write **SL** next to the words or phrases that describe your **Spiritual Life,** **S** next to anything related to the **Social** area of your life, **E** for words and phrases connected to who you are **Emotionally,** **I** for descriptions of who you are **Intellectually,** and **P** for comments relating to your **Physical being** [your appearance, physical abilities, health, etc.]. You might mark one word or phrase more than once, if applicable to different areas of life. Notice the area for which you wrote the most descriptive words or phrases. Why do you think you focused more on that area than the others?

_____

_____

_____

_____

_____

_____

_____

_____

_____

_____

℘ ♋

Look for yourself, and you will find in the long run only hatred, loneliness, despair, rage, ruin, and decay. But look for Christ and you will find Him, and with Him everything else thrown in.[69]

C.S. Lewis

℘ ♋

This week, we are considering the third focus of core healing, **Identity.** Take time to simply pause and wonder to what extent your self-perspective has been shaped by the molestation you experienced. As you continue becoming aware of who you are, realize that past influences can continue shaping how you see yourself until you consciously choose to change your perspective. We all have "automatic" thoughts, as described in chapter three. Living in the moment and, at the same time, being aware of new ways to tackle your concerns can help you avoid being stuck in old automatic negative thought patterns.

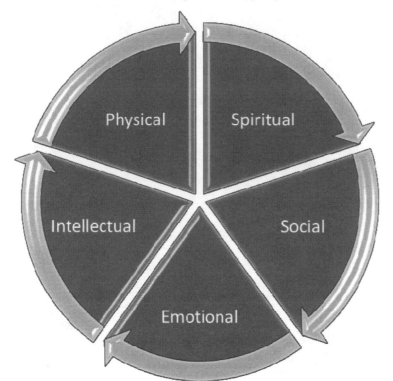

Life happens in five areas—spiritual, social, emotional, intellectual, and physical. Each of the five areas in the graph above is an important part of who you are and is vital to living a full and meaningful life. Since survivors of sexual abuse often "shut down," repress or deny legitimate needs and concerns, knowing who you are involves becoming fully alive in each area of life.

Do you notice yourself "shutting down" in any of the above areas? If so, describe how/when that occurs. _____

_____

_____

_____

_____

Core Healing Goal: to recognize five areas of identity and learn how to grow in each area.

1. Day One: **Discovering a Spiritual Identity**

   Often people say "I'm trying to find myself." When asked to explain how they will know when they have completed that mission, some respond with, "I will find myself in myself." That quest easily results in disillusionment and hopelessness, because we were not designed to find ourselves in ourselves. We were designed to find ourselves in God.

The idea of finding yourself in God might be a new idea to you, or it could be something you already believe. Please consider the following statements regarding spiritual identity:

Jesus said, *Come to Me, all you who labor and are heavy-laden and overburdened, and I will cause you to rest. [I will ease and relieve and refresh your souls.]* Matthew 11:28, AMP

Jesus said to him, I am the Way and the Truth and the Life; no one comes to the Father except by (through) Me. John 14:6, AMP

St. Augustine's *Confessions* begins "Great art Thou, O Lord and greatly to be praised...Thou hast made us for Thyself, O Lord, and our hearts are restless until they rest in Thee."

In his book *Mere Christianity*, C. S. Lewis stated, "What Satan put into the heads of our remote ancestors was the idea that they could 'be like gods'—could set up on their own as if they had created themselves—be their own masters—invent some sort of happiness for themselves outside God, apart from God. And out of that hopeless attempt has come nearly all that we call human history—money, poverty, ambition, war, prostitution, classes, empires, slavery—the long terrible story of man trying to find something other than God which will make him happy."[70]

As you consider the quotes above, write a response, as though you are talking directly with the author of each statement.

Jesus Christ: _____
_____
_____
_____

St. Augustine: _____
_____
_____
_____

C. S. Lewis: _____
_____
_____
_____
_____

℘ ℭ

The accuser says, "Feel guilty and condemned for all the great things the Most High has had to do for you." Deliberately refuse to listen to him. Because the more you listen, the more he'll say.[71]

Beth Moore

℘ ℭ

In an e-mail, a former client who is completing graduate work abroad shared her perspective about discovering identity.

Today I read the first chapter of john and was amazed how john the baptist answered those who questioned him about his own identity. He starts out by saying who he is not (sometimes it's easier to know who we are not, than who we are): he is not elijah nor the messiah, and then he defines himself as "the voice who calls out in the desert, prepare the way of the lord" - he is therefore completely defined by his mission.

I myself find strength in this because i literally have no other identity besides my mission in God's service. I don't feel like i have one nationality, a country, a home, not even a Christian denomination. The only home I have is heaven, and with God's help i will discover more of His will for me in this life.

As you consider your spiritual identity, have you thought of who you are in conjunction with the mission God has for your life? _____ Yes _____ No Explain. _____

_____

_____

_____

_____

_____

To help discover your unique spiritual mission, notice whether any obstacles are blocking your view of God's love. One obstacle that presents numerous challenges for survivors of abuse is difficulty trusting anyone, including God. Yet the Bible encourages us to, *"Trust in the Lord with all your heart, and lean not on your own understanding; in all your ways acknowledge Him, and He shall direct your paths"* (Proverbs 3:5-6, NKJV).

As you think about Proverbs 3:5-6, can you imagine yourself trusting God?
____ Yes ___ No   If so, describe ways you can tangibly trust in Him today. If not, describe the challenges you're experiencing: _____

_____

_____

_____

_____

_____

_____

A second obstacle to trusting in or relying on God could be either an attitude of stubborn rebellion or one of passive indifference toward Him, which the Bible refers to as sin. All of us have sinned, according to Romans 3:23 and Romans 6:23.

> So Cg
>
> In new birth, God reclaims what is rightfully His. He redirects the natural skills and abilities that Satan perverted and employs them for the completion of His plans and purposes.[72]
>
> Myles Munroe
>
> So Cg

94

The good news is that Jesus is God's provision for our sin. *"In this is love, not that we loved God, but that He loved us and sent His Son to be the propitiation for our sins. Beloved, if God so loved us, we also ought to love one another"* (1 John 4:10-11, NKJV).

1 John 4:10-11 describes two important concepts: the first (propitiation) is that Jesus paid for all of our sins. The second is that we are to love each other. When our spiritual life is as God designed it to be, we will learn how to relate effectively with other people. In other words, we will treat other people with God's limitless love when we experience that love ourselves.

Survivors of sexual abuse often feel singled out for rejection and hurt rather than love and acceptance. In contrast, Jesus overcomes rejection with love.

 Explore - *But Jesus went to the Mount of Olives. At dawn he appeared again in the temple courts, where all the people gathered around him, and he sat down to teach them. The teachers of the law and the Pharisees brought in a woman caught in adultery. They made her stand before the group and said to Jesus, "Teacher, this woman was caught in the act of adultery. In the Law Moses commanded us to stone such women. Now what do you say?" They were using this question as a trap, in order to have a basis for accusing him. But Jesus bent down and started to write on the ground with his finger. When they kept on questioning him, he straightened up and said to them, "If any one of you is without sin, let him be the first to throw a stone at her." Again he stooped down and wrote on the ground. At this, those who heard began to go away one at a time, the older ones first, until only Jesus was left, with the woman still standing there. Jesus straightened up and asked her, "Woman, where are they? Has no one condemned you?"*

"No one, sir," she said. "Then neither do I condemn you," Jesus declared. "Go now and leave your life of sin."

John 8:1-11, NIV

Do you think the woman "caught in adultery" could have been a survivor of sexual abuse? ____ Yes ____ No

Write your impressions about this incident. _____

_____

_____

_____

_____

_____

_____

_____

_____

_____

&ᖇ ᘯଓ

Bask in the luxury of being fully understood and unconditionally loved. Dare to see yourself as I [Jesus] see you: radiant in My righteousness, cleansed by My blood. I view you as the one I created you to be, the one you will be in actuality when heaven becomes your home. It is My Life within you that is changing you...[73]

Sarah Young

&ᖇ ᘯଓ

The religious leaders were using the woman to entrap Jesus; her well-being didn't matter to them at all. In contrast, Jesus treated her with dignity and respect. In verse 6, when Jesus *"bent down and started to write on the ground with his finger,"* many Bible scholars believe He was writing down specific sins of the religious leaders who wanted to stone the unidentified woman.

Beginning with the older men, after seeing what Jesus wrote on the ground and hearing Him say, *"If any one of you is without sin, let him be the first to throw a stone at her,"* the Pharisees dropped their stones to the ground. Instead of allowing them to condemn the woman, Jesus made every man face his own sin. One by one, the Pharisees walked away, leaving Jesus alone with the woman.

Jesus asked her, "Woman, where are they? Has no one condemned you?" She said, "No one, sir." Not only did Jesus show her He didn't condemn her; He gave the woman something proactive to do: "Go now and leave your life of sin."

As you see how Jesus treated this woman, can you imagine His love for you? ____ Yes ____ No Explain. _____
_____
_____
_____

Can you hear God speaking to you? He says: *I have loved you with an everlasting love; I have drawn you with loving-kindness.* Jeremiah 31:3, NIV

As you consider Jeremiah 31:3, what are you experiencing?

_____
_____
_____
_____
_____

Notice your emotional response to reading that God loves you "with an everlasting love." If you feel cynical or hurt by God's declaration of love for you, it could be because of *how* you're hearing His voice. Pause for a moment and think about this.

Sometimes survivors of sexual abuse hear God speak in the voice of their perpetrators—or in the harsh, demanding cruel voice of someone else who physically or emotionally abused them. If you realize you have been hearing a harsh, cruel "voice" of someone else and confusing that with God's voice, allow yourself to change how you hear God. His voice is kind, tender and compassionate; His voice is not cruel, oppressive or domineering.

So now there is no condemnation for those who belong to Christ Jesus. And because you belong to him, the power of the life-giving Spirit has freed you from the power of sin that leads to death.

Romans 8:1-2, NLT

God cares about your pain; He wants to rescue you from your past. How are you hearing His "voice"? _____

_____

_____

_____

For he will deliver the needy when he cries for help, the afflicted also, and him who has no helper. He will have compassion on the poor and needy, and the lives of the needy he will save. He will rescue their life from oppression and violence, and their blood will be precious in his sight...

Psalm 72:12-14, NASU

If you have not already done so, you can accept Jesus' payment for your sins and leave them in the past, as well as each of the sins done against you by others. When you do, you begin moving forward into a new future and new hope. You can begin to enjoy God today—and continue the process forever. You can even ask God to give you new desires, hopes and dreams. Consider the psalmist's encouragement:

Delight yourself in the Lord; and He will give you the desires of your heart. Psalm 37:4, NASU

As you continue core healing in your spiritual identity, will you make Psalm 37:4 your prayer?_____ Yes _____ No   If you answered "yes," rewrite Psalm 37:4 in your own words. If you answered, "no," write about the ways in which it is still difficult for you to trust God. _____

_____

_____

_____

_____

_____

_____

_____

2. Day Two: **Social Identity**

Some survivors of sexual abuse feel unable to function in social settings. Many feel "different" from others. Others say they have felt unaccepted, unlovable or unattractive since their sexual abuse began. Feeling "branded" by invisible trauma, many unknowingly (but voluntarily) give their perpetrator power to define them for the rest of their lives.

As you consider who you are **socially**, do you notice any areas in which your perpetrator still controls how you think, feel or behave? [Hint: if you avoid

Seeing then that we have a great High Priest who has passed through the heavens, Jesus the Son of God, let us hold fast our confession. For we do not have a High Priest who cannot sympathize with our weaknesses, but was in all points tempted as we are, yet without sin. Let us therefore come boldly to the throne of grace, that we may obtain mercy and find grace to help in time of need.

Hebrews 4:14-16, NKJV

people, believe you don't "fit in," or measure your worth by what you think others are thinking about you, your predator could be defining your present.] List any areas that come to mind. _____

_____

You can change your social identity by making new choices every day. Dr. Kevin Leman writes, "If you've learned to become the product of your environment, you can unlearn the negative aspects and build on the positive ones."[72]

Notice how you view yourself, and then think about how God views you. (Read Psalm 139 to see His perspective.) How might looking at yourself with a fresh perspective help you relate more effectively with others than you do now?

_____

_____

_____

_____

_____

What internal labels do you give yourself when you try [and sometimes fail] to fit in with others? [Do you call yourself names like "inept, toxic, stupid, misfit, unlovable"?]

_____

_____

_____

Would you speak to anyone else as unkindly as you talk to yourself in your thoughts? _____ Yes _____ No Explain. _____

_____

_____

Write down healing labels you will say [think] to yourself, making a choice to develop optimistic perspectives about yourself. These new thoughts can go with you to any social setting.

_____

_____

_____

_____

Often survivors of sexual abuse are able to mask their real emotions socially, looking happy, strong, secure, and confident—until they get home. Then their children, spouse or close friends see a different person. Anger,

ஐ ௧

If you've learned to become the product of your environment, you can unlearn the negative aspects and build on the positive ones.[74]

Dr. Kevin Leman

ஐ ௧

depression (which is often anger turned inward), or insecurity can come out in myriad different ways.

Are you the same person everywhere you go? _____ Yes _____ No If not, describe how and where differences in your behavior occur.

_____

_____

_____

_____

_____

_____

_____

_____

_____

_____

_____

_____

_____

_____

_____

_____

Instead of giving up in discouragement about challenges you have relating with people, you can be proactive. For example, if you vent toxic anger on immediate family members, please deal with your anger and begin building healthy relationships with them before developing other relationships.

At the end of this chapter is a list of books that can help with various challenges.

The main thing to remember regarding your social identity is that you can choose now **not** to let the past continue dictating how you relate with others. Look for activities in your area that you could enjoy—such as fitness classes, Bible studies, volunteering at a hospital or hospice, taking meals to people who are ill, or helping in an outreach, such as a homeless shelter.

You don't have to wait for someone to ask you; you can volunteer. And if the first, second, or third group you choose doesn't need volunteers, keep looking and praying about where you can use the gifts you have been given to help others. (Chapter Ten will continue this discussion.)

ৎৄ ৫৩

When you have to make a choice and don't make it, that is in itself a choice.[75]

William James

ৎৄ ৫৩

What positive steps will you take, beginning today? _____

_____

_____

_____

_____

_____

_____

_____

_____

3. Day Three: **Emotional Identity**

To help see yourself as a valued emotional being, you need to consciously let go of old attitudes that simply cannot help you get where you want to go. One false belief that can keep you trapped in the past is the idea that you have to "feel good" before you can heal.

Instead of focusing on changing your feelings, focus on adjusting how you think. Consciously choosing new thought processes can result in significant changes in your emotions and moods. [Refer to chapter three, "Don't Believe Everything You Think," and Appendix A for practical ideas.]

On the other hand, it is important to be aware of your feelings—and allow yourself to feel rather than "numbing out" as you might have done in the past. Just as indicator lights on the dashboard of a car remind you of things you need to deal with, your feelings can help you notice when something is wrong, add depth and joy to life and help you become aware of areas of life where change and growth need to occur. On the following page is a **Continuum of Emotions**. Notice the six secondary emotions in bold letters at either end of a continuum. Each of these emotions is fueled by other feelings.

To be aware of the continuum, consider a few of anger's triggers. Often when we say "I am angry," it is because we feel hurt, frustrated, irritated, resentful, jealous, controlled, etc. It is important to learn to identify what is really going on, noticing and dealing with root causes, yet not being controlled by them but by God and His limitless love.

When you feel angry, you can apply Ephesians 4, remembering you are free in Christ and can release your anger to Him after you initially experience it.

In your anger do not sin: Do not let the sun go down while you are still angry, and do not give the devil a foothold. (Ephesians 4:26-27, NIV)

How can you apply what Ephesians 4:26-27 teaches about anger? _____

_____

_____

On the Continuum of Emotions, below, three positive emotions listed on the right contrast with the three challenging emotions noted on the left. When you feel angry, depressed or anxious, your choices can move your emotions to a calm, joyful or safe status.

Be careful not to ignore challenging emotions. For example, there are many times you need to allow yourself to feel depressed—such as when you have experienced a loss. Not allowing yourself to feel buries true emotions, which can cause significant difficulties. When you feel anxious, look for the source of the anxiety and then take practical steps to trust God with your concerns while doing what you need to do to address issues, events and challenges.

Continuum of Emotions

Circle the **WORDS** *that apply to you in each list below.* (Note: the words on either end of the continuum are opposites or extremes.)

ANGRY   BITTER   FRUSTRATED   RESPECTED   EMPOWERED   **CALM**
⟵——————————————————————————————⟶

What other words (such as hurt, furious, jealous, cheated, resentful, offended OR loved, appreciated, valued, complete, open, forgiven, etc.) describe where you are on the anger continuum? _____

_____

_____

DEPRESSED   HOPELESS   ALONE   CREATIVE   GRATEFUL   **JOYFUL**
⟵——————————————————————————————⟶

What other words (despair, humiliated, sad, empty, guilty, ashamed, worthless, inferior, OR hopeful, alive, connected, enthusiastic, etc.) show where you are on the depressed continuum? _____

_____

_____

ANXIOUS   OVERWHELMED   VULNERABLE   CONFIDENT   RELAXED   **SAFE**
⟵——————————————————————————————⟶

When you are experiencing fear and anxiety, what other words (worried, paralyzed, helpless, rejected, numb; OR trusting, secure, understood, encouraged, protected, etc.) describe where you are on this continuum? ____

_____

_____

_____

ଘ ଓ
_____

Be careful not to ignore challenging emotions. Not allowing yourself to feel suppresses true emotions and can cause significant difficulties.
_____

ଘ ଓ

Besides noticing root causes of emotions, you need to be aware of emotional obstacles to healing, such as unconscious defense mechanisms. Your emotional infrastructure automatically activated various emotional defense procedures to help you cope with the trauma of sexual abuse.

Emotional defense mechanisms are similar to the physiological "fight or flight" response. [When people are attacked physically, they either fight back or flee from their assailants.] Emotional defense mechanisms protected you from experiencing emotions you were not designed to bear. Though they were a necessary response for your survival at the time of your abuse, remaining in defense mode is neither helpful nor conducive to healing.

You can begin to recognize what, if any, defense mechanisms are still in place and intentionally replace them with new responses that can benefit your restorative progress. Since you are no longer facing the stressors that activated these defense mechanisms, it is not helpful for you to keep using them in daily life. [Notice defense mechanisms that are activated to distance yourself from awareness of difficult thoughts, feelings and behaviors, such as anxiety or interpersonal conflict.]

After you consider the defense mechanisms listed below and on the following page, place a check next to those you are currently using [✓], then describe how you have utilized various defense mechanisms to "defend yourself" from the pain of your past.

[ ] Denial [not acknowledging what really happened; rejecting a disturbing thought or feeling; disregarding or ignoring a frightening reality] _____

_____

_____

[ ] Repression [involuntary removal of traumatic events from conscious awareness; instinctively placing painful memories in subconscious mind] ___

_____

_____

[ ] Blame [denying responsibility for making new choices to grow while blaming challenges you're facing on others instead of actively looking for solutions] _____

_____

_____

[ ] Intellectualism [using intellectual arguments to explain your current concerns and failing to acknowledge your responsibility for current feelings; reading book after book to find new intellectual answers without taking conscious steps to change and grow] _____

_____

_____

ॐ ✿

Emotional defense mechanisms protected you from experiencing emotions you were not designed to bear. Though they were a necessary response for your survival at the time of your abuse, remaining in defense mode is not conducive to healing.

ॐ ✿

102

[ ] Humor [in itself humor can be helpful; it is not helpful as a defense mechanism when used to deflect deep conversations and/or internal awareness or keeps you from acknowledging and addressing pain] _____

_____

_____

[ ] Trivializing/Minimizing [e.g. "Oh, my abuse wasn't so bad; hers was a lot worse"—not admitting the depth of your pain or your need to heal] _____

_____

_____

[ ] Projection [attributing your unwanted thoughts, feelings, or actions to someone else, e.g., thinking "She hates me!" when you really aren't accepting yourself] _____

_____

_____

_____

[ ] Exhibiting anger [blowing up at others who try to draw you out; or internalizing rage, denying your feelings of bitterness with rationalization—coming up with explanations to justify yourself while ignoring how you feel]

_____

_____

_____

Write down three or four words that describe how you think others would describe your personality: _____

_____

_____

Review Psalm 139, and then imagine allowing yourself to be the person God created you to be, fully expressing your unique personality with joy and passion. If someone else were able to see you as an authentic emotional being, what would s/he see? _____

_____

_____

_____

_____

_____

_____

_____

ℬ ℭ

How precious also are Your thoughts to me, O God! How great is the sum of them! If I should count them, they would be more in number than the sand; When I awake, I am still with You.

Psalm 139:17-18, NKJV

ℬ ℭ

God has something better for you than anything the world offers. In John 15:9-12, Jesus says, *"I've loved you the way my Father has loved me. Make yourselves at home in my love. If you keep my commands, you'll remain intimately at home in my love. That's what I've done — kept my Father's commands and made myself at home in his love. I've told you these things for a purpose: that my joy might be your joy, and your joy wholly mature. This is my command: Love one another the way I loved you"* (The Message).

If you have shut down emotionally, you are robbing not only yourself of the love and joy God offers you; you are also robbing others of the joy of knowing the "you" God created you to be. What, if anything, is stopping you from accepting God's gift of joy and love? _____

_____

_____

_____

_____

_____

₧ ₨

Emotionally healthy spirituality is about reality, not denial or illusion.[76]

Peter Scazzero

₧ ₨

One emotion that keeps many people "stuck" is guilt. If you are experiencing guilt, pause to wonder whether it is false guilt or real guilt. False guilt keeps you in a repetitive state of self-condemnation and blame, with no lasting escape. Real guilt could better be termed "conviction," a state in which the Holy Spirit convicts you of an attitude or action that can be changed. False guilt provides condemnation and no way out. When God convicts you of something, He provides the way out. *If we confess our sins, He is faithful and righteous to forgive us our sins and to cleanse us from all unrighteousness.* 1 John 1:9, NASU

How can you apply 1 John 1:9 to your concerns? _____

_____

_____

_____

_____

_____

Did you notice that God promises to cleanse us from all unrighteousness? The Amplified version of 1 John 1:9 says, *"If we [freely] admit that we have sinned and confess our sins, He is faithful and just (true to His own nature and promises) and will forgive our sins [dismiss our lawlessness] and [continuously] cleanse us from all unrighteousness [everything not in conformity to His will in purpose, thought, and action]."*

As you consider 1 John 1:9 in both translations, do you notice that it's God's job to cleanse us from everything that needs to be changed in our lives? It's our job to allow Him to do His magnificent work.

Take a few moments to consider and write about the utter freedom God provides from guilt. _____

_____

_____

_____

_____

_____

4. Day Four: **Intellectual Identity**

Some go into overdrive in one area of life. For many, it's far easier to continue achieving academic degrees than it is to feel emotional pain. (You might recall from Day Three that Intellectualism can be an emotional defense mechanism.)

Do you push yourself to succeed academically so much that you neglect to take time to relax and enjoy life? ____ Yes ____ No Explain: _____

_____

_____

There is absolutely nothing wrong with succeeding academically; in fact, it is a great idea to continue learning and growing throughout life. The point here is to simply notice your motive. Are you facing your past, dealing with it and moving forward in life, or are you letting any activity stop you from internal change and growth? _____

_____

_____

What might it look like if you gave yourself intellectual permission to recognize the pain of your past so you can let it go? _____

_____

_____

_____

_____

It is also vital to realize that the pain of your past is not who you are. You are a complex being, created in the image of God, imbued with value, dignity and strength.

David G. Benner states, "Before we can surrender ourselves we must become ourselves, for no one can give up what he or she does not first possess... Before we can become our self we must accept our self, just as we are. Self-acceptance always precedes genuine self-surrender and self-transformation."[77]

> ✦ ✦
>
> *Christ has set us free to live a free life. So take your stand! Never again let anyone put a harness of slavery on you.*
>
> Galatians 5:1, THE MESSAGE
>
> ✦ ✦

"...if you're content to be simply yourself, you will become more than yourself" (Luke 18:14, THE MESSAGE).

What would it look like for you "to become more than yourself"? _____

_____

_____

_____

_____

_____

_____

Explore - *The Lord your God is in your midst, a victorious warrior. He will exult over you with joy, He will be quiet in His love, He will rejoice over you with shouts of joy.* Zephaniah 3:17 (NASU)

In this verse, Zephaniah is describing God's perspective of you. Using your intellect to acknowledge your worth is an important step in your healing journey. Write what you are learning about your intrinsic value: _____

_____

_____

_____

_____

_____

_____

_____

Your mind can help you retrain every area of your life! The apostle Paul explains how to choose what you think.

Since, then, you have been raised with Christ, set your hearts on things above, where Christ is seated at the right hand of God. Set your minds on things above, not on earthly things. For you died, and your life is now hidden with Christ in God. When Christ, who is your life, appears, then you also will appear with him in glory. Colossians 3:1-4, NIV

In Colossians 3:1-4, where does it say to "set" your heart? _____

And where does it say to "set" your mind? _____

What rationale does Paul give for choosing to focus on something other than what is happening on earth? _____

_____

_____

_____

In Philippians, Paul records some of his many intellectual qualifications. *"But whatever was to my profit I now consider loss for the sake of Christ. What is more, I consider everything a loss compared to the surpassing greatness of knowing Christ Jesus my Lord, for whose sake I have lost all things. I consider them rubbish, that I may gain Christ and be found in him, not having a righteousness of my own that comes from the law, but that which is through faith in Christ—the righteousness that comes from God and is by faith. I want to know Christ and the power of his resurrection and the fellowship of sharing in his sufferings..."* (Philippians 3:7-10a, NIV).

In what ways did Paul feel knowing Christ was more valuable than his personal achievements? _____

_____

_____

_____

_____

Read 2 Corinthians 10:4-5 and use the space below to describe what we are told to do with our thoughts, explaining what "to take captive" means to you.

The weapons we fight with are not the weapons of the world. On the contrary, they have divine power to demolish strongholds. We demolish arguments and every pretension that sets itself up against the knowledge of God, and we take captive every thought to make it obedient to Christ. 2 Corinthians 10:4-5, NIV

_____

_____

_____

_____

Paul was an intellectual—fluent in numerous languages, a world traveler and a spiritual leader. Why do you think he saw a need to yield his thought processes to Christ? _____

_____

_____

_____

How has today's work helped you value or direct your intellectual identity?

_____

_____

_____

_____

All the attributes of Christ, as God and man, are at our disposal. All the fulness of the Godhead, whatever that marvellous term may comprehend, is ours to make us complete. He cannot endow us with the attributes of Deity; but He has done all that can be done, for He has made even His divine power and Godhead subservient to our salvation.[79]

C.H. Spurgeon

The heart is hopelessly dark and deceitful, a puzzle that no one can figure out. But I, God, search the heart and examine the mind. I get to the heart of the human. I get to the root of things. I treat them as they really are, not as they pretend to be."

Jeremiah 17:9-10, THE MESSAGE

We are holistic people, with all areas of our lives intertwined. What parts of who you are do you see in Jeremiah 17: 9-10? _____

_____

_____

_____

_____

_____

_____

_____

Whose job is it to search and examine your mind and heart? _____

Will you ask God to help you as you continue your healing journey?
____ Yes ____ No Journal your response: _____

_____

_____

_____

_____

_____

_____

_____

_____

_____

_____

_____

_____

If you have intellectual questions about believing in God, you may want to read one of the books listed at the end of the chapter under "Validity of Your Faith."

New feelings of resentment surfaced. "How could my parents have done those horrible things to me?" she [Glenda] thought. "I was just a little girl. Why didn't they let me be a little girl? I was beaten, stripped, molested, cursed, screamed at, kicked, and hated when all I ever wanted was love. I would have done anything for their love."[80]

Joni Eareckson Tada

5. Day Five: **Physical Identity**

An overemphasis on our bodies—how they look, smell, and feel; what they can achieve and who they're walking around with—confuses us. Too much preoccupation with our bodies can actually increase physical problems. Yet, not paying attention to or understanding the way our bodies work can have disastrous results.

One challenge faced by some survivors of sexual abuse is referred to in the DSM-IV as "somatization disorder."[81] Individuals experiencing somatization disorder can present numerous complex, diverse medical complaints that could be rooted in the emotional trauma of molestation. Certainly one should not ignore physical symptoms. But if you have various physical complaints that physicians cannot seem to help, it could be time to consult a mental health professional to see if any of your physical symptoms have an emotional basis that can be addressed with appropriate counseling.

In his book "The Stress of Life," Hans Selye, M.D. explained that most people fail to realize that "knowing what hurts you has an inherent curative value....The tweezers of stress have three prongs. Whether we suffer from a boil on the skin, a disease of the kidney, or a troubled mind, careful study of the condition will usually reveal it to consist of three major elements: 1) The stressor, the external agent which started the trouble; 2) The defensive measures, such as hormones and nervous stimuli which encourage the body to defend itself against the stressor as well as it can; 3) The mechanisms for surrender, such as hormonal and nervous stimuli, which encourage the body not to defend itself." He writes that "we can often eliminate the stressor ourselves, once we have recognized its nature, or we can adjust the proportion between active defensive attitudes and measures of surrender, in the best interest of maintaining our balance."[82]

We looked at defense mechanisms earlier in this chapter. Are there any ways you can reduce your stress by simply encouraging your body to relax rather than "defending" itself? _____

_____

_____

_____

_____

_____

_____

_____

_____

_____

_____

> ℘ ℭ
>
> The true self is who you are becoming. It is not something you need to construct through a process of self improvement or deconstruct by means of psychological analysis. Rather, it is your total self as you were created by God and as you are being redeemed in Christ. It is the image of God that you are— the unique face of God that has been set aside from eternity for you.[83]
>
> David G. Benner
>
> ℘ ℭ

To help you understand the intricate creation of the human and spiritual body, read *Fearfully and Wonderfully Made* by British surgeon Dr. Paul Brand and American author Philip Yancey. This book will help you appreciate the magnificent intricacy of your body. (This book is available in a Spanish edition: *Temerosa Y Maravillosamente Diseñado*.)

You can quit living in defense mode and begin to enjoy living. For many, though, the area of sexual intimacy is the one physical area they don't have any hope of changing.

Intimacy is often a profoundly challenging area for survivors of sexual abuse. Some people have little interest in sexuality; others have almost an insatiable appetite for sexual acts but little capacity for intimate emotional and spiritual connection. It is important that you reclaim who you are as a sexual being, discovering God's perfect design for your body. Recommended books for further study are included at the end of this chapter.

How you talk to yourself about your sexuality can transform how you see yourself in this important area. Someone said, "The brain is the main sexual organ." You can tell yourself, "Intimacy with my spouse is not sexual abuse; I can enjoy safe touches now; I can say what feels good and what doesn't feel good—and expect my spouse to respect me, not molest me."

When you were molested, your abuser overpowered you for selfish gain. Your abuser committed criminal behavior. There was no intimacy involved. Now that you are safe, you can learn that true sexual intimacy is different. When a sexual touch triggers physical sensations that remind you of abuse, you can tell yourself, "I am here now. I am not there. I am safe now. I am learning God's true design." Reading the Song of Solomon can help you see God's beautiful design for sexual intimacy. You don't have to be robbed of the joy for which God designed your sexuality.

You can learn how to be whole physically—and in every other area of your life. Write down how you can reclaim your body according to God's design.

_____

_____

_____

_____

_____

_____

_____

_____

_____

_____

ಸಂ ಲ

Cling to God's hand, follow His lead, and allow Him to heal you. Before you know it, you'll be nearing the end of the dark tunnel and the freedom found in that light up ahead.[84]

Nicole Braddock Bromley

ಸಂ ಲ

Week Eight - Weekend Bonus Work

The sixth stage of psychosocial development, Later Adolescence, occurs from ages 18 through 24. The central process of development in this stage is role experimentation, which includes participating in a variety of roles until deciding what one prefers.[85] Experimentation could lead to discovering a course of study, career path or future marriage partner. Some Western cultures encourage experimentation in diverse gender roles, which can result in profound confusion. Molestation during or prior to this developmental stage could seriously impact a person's perceptions of his or her sexual identity.

Consider one woman's experience during Later Adolescence.

Sabrina was a college student when she came for counseling to heal from sexual abuse that began at about age 5, during Early School Age.

During one of her sessions, Sabrina nervously asked, "Could I be a lesbian?" Listening, observing her anxiety, I asked if anything had happened recently that caused her concern.

She explained, "My friend was brushing my hair the other day, and I felt tingly all over; it felt really good. I told my friend how it felt, and she said, 'That means you're a lesbian, like me.'"

I responded, "Most people feel good when their hair is brushed, particularly since hair and scalp is an erogenous zone. You can experience sensual stimulation there similar to feelings people have in other erogenous zones, such as lips, genitals and breasts."

Sabrina said that she didn't know that having hair touched could cause those sensations. She then asked, "Does that mean I'm not a lesbian?"

I asked what she thought.

With obvious relief, Sabrina smiled and said, "I like guys; I don't think I'm gay; I just thought...since my friend said that; I must be..."

We talked about how being molested during Early School Age, when gender identity is being formed, could create confusion in one's thinking about gender identity.

Sabrina relaxed, stating with confidence, "I'm not a lesbian."

If a therapist had told Sabrina, "Yes, feeling tingly all over when your friend brushed your hair must mean you're gay," she could have been coerced to believe her identity was something clearly different from what it is—and different from what she desired. Instead, she is able to enjoy being the woman God created her to be.

During Later Adolescence, people learn to be faithful to values they embrace and loyal to the people close to them. In relativistic cultures, that presents a serious challenge. Since many are told there are no absolutes, their values shift with cultural whims. Interestingly enough, the person stating "there are no absolutes" is declaring an absolute. Take time today to consider the freedom God offers to experience lasting loyalty through His unfailing love.

୫୦ ଓଃ

Molestation during or prior to Later Adolescence could seriously impact a person's perceptions of his or her sexual identity.

୫୦ ଓଃ

BRAIN FUNCTIONS

Amen, Daniel G., M.D. – "Change Your Brain, Change Your Life: The Breakthrough Program for Conquering Anxiety, Depression, Obsessiveness, Anger, and Impulsiveness" (Three Rivers Press)

Henslin, Dr. Earl and Amen, Daniel, M.D. – "This Is Your Brain on Joy" (Thomas Nelson)

INTERPERSONAL RELATIONSHIPS

Benner, David G. – "The Gift of Being Yourself: The Sacred Call to Self-Discovery" (IVP Books)

Carter, Dr. Les and Minirth, Dr. Frank – "The Anger Workbook," (Nelson)

Chapman, Dr. Gary – "The 5 Love Languages" (Zondervan)

Cloud, Dr. Henry and Townsend, Dr. John – "Safe People" (Zondervan)

Smalley, Dr. Gary – "The DNA of Relationships" (Tyndale)

Wibbels, Alan & Marti – "Relationships Pure and Simple: A Biblical Perspective on Relationships"

INTIMACY

Penner, Dr. Clifford and Joyce – "The Gift of Sex: A Christian Guide to Sexual Fulfillment" (W Publishing Group)

Rosenau, Dr. Douglas E. – "A Celebration of Sex: A Guide to Enjoying God's Gift of Sexual Intimacy" (Thomas Nelson)

Wheat, Ed M.D. and Wheat, Gaye – "Intended for Pleasure" (Revell)

PHYSICAL NEEDS

Brand, Dr. Paul and Yancey, Philip – "Fearfully and Wonderfully Made" (Zondervan) – (also available in Spanish, "Temerosa Y Maravillosamente Diseñado")

Selye, Dr. Hans – "The Stress of Life" (McGraw-Hill)

Swensen, Richard A., M.D. – "Margin" (NavPress).

VALIDITY OF YOUR FAITH

McDowell, Josh – "The New Evidence That Demands a Verdict" (Thomas Nelson)

Strobel, Lee – "The Case for Christ: a Journalist's Personal Investigation of the Evidence for Jesus" (Zondervan)

Our identity should be seen as an ongoing process. Rather than a static snapshot, we should embrace a flowing sense of self, whereby we are perpetually re-framing, re-organizing, re-thinking and re-considering ourselves. How different would life be if rather than asking who I am, we contemplated how we'd like to engage life.[86]

Mel Schwartz, L.C.S.W

Designed with Purpose

Chapter Nine

When you are confident that your life matters, everything else in life comes into perspective. Throughout this book, you have learned that you are valuable and that you are no longer defined by the abuse that damaged your innermost being. Now it is time to heal in another core area, **Purpose**.

What is purpose? In his manifesto on the meaning of life, Rick Warren stated, "The purpose of your life is far greater than your own personal fulfillment, your peace of mind, or even your happiness. It's far greater than your family, your career, or even your wildest dreams and ambitions. If you want to know why you were placed on this planet, you must begin with God. You were born *by* His purpose and *for* His purpose." [87]

Core Healing Goal: to understand and articulate your life purpose.

1. Day One: **Finding Focus**

    Are you focusing on personal fulfillment, peace of mind, happiness, success or something other than God? _____ Yes _____ No   If yes, what specific goal(s) are you trying to reach? _____

    _____

    _____

    _____

    Think about where you invest your time, energy, and resources. Write a sentence that summarizes your current passion or life focus. _____

    _____

    _____

    _____

> ℰℴ ℭℬ
>
> The world, for the most part, assumes you are something to be molded or manipulated... Our contention is that you have a design of your own—God's blueprint—and can only be fulfilled when you carry out that design, regardless of how high or low on the ladder of success you are. [89]
>
> Arthur F. Miller & Ralph T. Mattson
>
> ℰℴ ℭℬ

In his book "In Pursuit of Purpose," Myles Monroe focuses on the unique contributions that only your life can make. "Your existence is evidence that this generation needs something that your life contains. ...you were born *for* a purpose and *with* a purpose. *Your personal fulfillment is possible only in so far as you complete your destiny.* The discovery of your personal purpose and its relationship to God's universal purpose must be the basis from which you live. *You must strive to be who you were born to be.*" [88]

If you experienced interruptions to the purpose for which you were born, it is vital to know that real meaning can begin now, with God your Creator. The psalmist describes His amazing creation of you in Psalm 139.

Explore - *For You formed my inward parts; You wove me in my mother's womb. I will give thanks to You, for I am fearfully and wonderfully made; wonderful are Your works, and my soul knows it very well. My frame was not hidden from You, when I was made in secret, and skillfully wrought in the depths of the earth; Your eyes have seen my unformed substance; and in Your book were all written the days that were ordained for me, when as yet there was not one of them.*

Psalm 139:13-16, NASU

Why did the psalmist thank God? _____
_____
_____

Pause for a moment and thank God for His creation of you and ask Him to begin to show you how He is going to use you to impact this generation. Record your insights here. _____
_____
_____
_____
_____
_____
_____

Today, there is an enormous emphasis on success (which is often defined as wealth, social prominence, beauty and/or achievement). Living by the world's definition of success is as elusive as capturing a shadow. Once you think you have it, you don't. Some people emphasize business expertise, while others call attention to educational competence or to the diverse accomplishments of one's extended family. If there is no one who seems to notice what you do or care who you are, how can you know your contributions to society have any meaning at all? _____
_____
_____
_____

ᔕ ᔐ

When anything in creation fulfills its purpose, it brings glory to God.[90]

Rick Warren

ᔕ ᔐ

Explore - You can know your worth without a shadow of doubt. God explains the value of your life in Matthew 6. *If you decide for God, living a life of God-worship, it follows that you don't fuss about what's on the table at mealtimes or whether the clothes in your closet are in fashion. There is far more to your life than the food you put in your stomach, more to your outer appearance than the clothes you hang on your body. Look at the birds, free and unfettered, not tied down to a job description, careless in the care of God. And you count far more to him than birds. Has anyone by fussing in front of the mirror ever gotten taller by so much as an inch? All this time and money wasted on*

fashion—do you think it makes that much difference? Instead of looking at the fashions, walk out into the fields and look at the wildflowers. They never primp or shop, but have you ever seen color and design quite like it? The ten best-dressed men and women in the country look shabby alongside them.

If God gives such attention to the appearance of wildflower—most of which are never even seen — don't you think he'll attend to you, take pride in you, do his best for you? What I'm trying to do here is to get you to relax, to not be so preoccupied with getting, so you can respond to God's giving. People who don't know God and the way he works fuss over these things, but you know both God and how he works. Steep your life in God-reality, God-initiative, God-provisions. Don't worry about missing out. You'll find all your everyday human concerns will be met.

Give your entire attention to what God is doing right now, and don't get worked up about what may or may not happen tomorrow. God will help you deal with whatever hard things come up when the time comes.

Matthew 6:25-34, THE MESSAGE

According to Matthew 6, how can you be "careless in the care of God," giving your full attention to what He is doing, living in the moment?

_____
_____
_____
_____
_____
_____

What does God promise to do when difficult things happen to you? _____

_____
_____
_____
_____
_____

Even amidst suffering, our lives can exhibit purpose. In his book "Man's Search for Meaning," Jewish psychiatrist Viktor Frankl wrote about the appalling horror he experienced as a prisoner of Nazi Germany during World War II. "Man *can* preserve a vestige of spiritual freedom, of independence of mind, even in such terrible conditions of psychic and physical stress. We who lived in concentration camps can remember the men who walked through the huts comforting others, giving away their last piece of bread. They may have been few in number, but they offer sufficient proof that everything can be taken from a man but one thing: the last of the human freedoms—to choose one's attitude in any given set of circumstances, to choose one's own way." [91]

Seek the Kingdom of God above all else, and live righteously, and he will give you everything you need.

Matthew 6:33, NLT

115

In what specific ways will you choose to have a purposeful attitude? _____

_____

_____

_____

_____

_____

_____

 Explore - *Therefore, I urge you, brothers, in view of God's mercy, to offer your bodies as living sacrifices, holy and pleasing to God—this is your spiritual act of worship. Do not conform any longer to the pattern of this world, but be transformed by the renewing of your mind. Then you will be able to test and approve what God's will is—his good, pleasing and perfect will.*

Romans 12:1-2, NIV

As you become aware of His mercy, what does God ask you to choose to do with your body? _____

_____

_____

_____

In order to keep from being conformed to the world, God asks you to renew your mind. How can your mind be renewed? What will you be able to "test and approve" when you allow your mind to be transformed? _____

_____

_____

_____

_____

Success in life is simply living in the power of the Holy Spirit and leaving the results to God. Journal about specific ways you can choose to walk in God's will and strength instead of conforming to the world's pattern. _____

_____

_____

_____

_____

_____

_____

_____

_____

_____

ଃଠ ଓଃ

Success in life is simply living in the power of the Holy Spirit and leaving the results to God.

ଃଠ ଓଃ

2. Day Two: **Doing Small Things Instead of Great Things**

Mother Teresa said, "In this life we cannot do great things. We can only do small things with great love."[92]

Although Mother Teresa completed many great achievements, she said, "We cannot do great things." She won a Nobel Peace Prize, yet she stated, "We can only do small things with great love." As a nun in India, she was so overwhelmed by the suffering she observed outside her convent's walls that she asked for permission to work with the people no one was helping. She devoted her life to helping the poorest of the poor in the slums of Calcutta. She spoke with presidents and kings; she made a difference in the world—and in the lives of the people she touched.

Her triumph began with noticing where the needs were. If we focus on our own needs, we cannot see the needs of others. Yet everyone has needs; everyone has significant struggles. Take time today to simply notice the people around you and prayerfully wonder what needs one other person might have. If you have an opportunity to ask someone about specific needs, do so. Write your thoughts or discoveries here. _____

_____

_____

_____

_____

_____

_____

 Explore - *Anyone who receives a prophet because he is a prophet will receive a prophet's reward, and anyone who receives a righteous man because he is a righteous man will receive a righteous man's reward. And if anyone gives even a cup of cold water to one of these little ones because he is my disciple, I tell you the truth, he will certainly not lose his reward.*

Matthew 10:41-42, NIV

As Jesus pointed out in the passage above, true ministry and purpose often happens when you don't even realize it. List several ways you can begin to give people "a cup of cold water," or any act of random kindness, expecting no return from the person to which you gave it. _____

_____

_____

_____

_____

_____

_____

ℬ ℭ

Take time today to simply notice the people around you and prayerfully wonder what needs one other person might have.

ℬ ℭ

Have you noticed how seldom people smile at each other in stores, at work, at home? Could one "small thing" you do today simply be smiling at another person? _____ Yes _____ No If you answered "yes" to this, write about what happens when you intentionally smile at someone. _____

_____

_____

_____

_____

Viktor Frankl taught that "we can discover meaning in life in three different ways: (1) by creating a work or doing a deed; (2) by experiencing something or encountering someone; and (3) by the attitude we take toward unavoidable suffering." [93]

When you were molested, you experienced incredible, undeserved suffering; you now recognize many of the challenges inherent in such trauma. Perhaps you are aware that you cannot always find peace in people, circumstances or even in the work you do. A repeated focus on the fact or pain of your suffering could leave you feeling trapped in the past. Instead, you can choose an attitude that moves you beyond your suffering. You can rely on God moment-by-moment for the authentic hope and healing He provides to everyone who trusts in Him.

Some people miss the joy of simply living because they are waiting to accomplish something "big." Charles Spurgeon addressed the significance of anything we do in Jesus' name, stating, "In all works of faith we may count upon Jesus' fellowship. It is when we are in His work that we may reckon upon His smile. Ye unknown workers who are occupied for your Lord amid the dirt and wretchedness of the lowest of the low, be of good cheer, for jewels have been found upon dunghills ere now, earthen pots have been filled with heavenly treasure, and ill weeds have been transformed into precious flowers. Dwell ye with the King for His work, and when He writes His chronicles your name shall be recorded."

How can you enjoy each moment today and appreciate Jesus' fellowship in whatever tasks you do? _____

_____

_____

_____

_____

The following passage summarizes how to discover meaning and purpose.

Explore - *Since Jesus went through everything you're going through and more, learn to think like him. Think of your sufferings as a weaning from that old sinful habit of always expecting to get your own*

₧ ₨

God wants to raise up people filled with hope. True hope is not rooted in my achievements or assets, but in my knowledge that I am the child of the King. [94]

Paul David Tripp

₧ ₨

way. Then you'll be able to live out your days free to pursue what God wants instead of being tyrannized by what you want.

You've already put in your time in that God-ignorant way of life, partying night after night, a drunken and profligate life. Now it's time to be done with it for good. Of course, your old friends don't understand why you don't join in with the old gang anymore. But you don't have to give an account to them. They're the ones who will be called on the carpet—and before God himself.

Listen to the Message. It was preached to those believers who are now dead, and yet even though they died (just as all people must), they will still get in on the life that God has given in Jesus.

Everything in the world is about to be wrapped up, so take nothing for granted. Stay wide-awake in prayer. Most of all, love each other as if your life depended on it. Love makes up for practically anything. Be quick to give a meal to the hungry, a bed to the homeless – cheerfully. Be generous with the different things God gave you, passing them around so all get in on it: if words, let it be God's words; if help, let it be God's hearty help. That way, God's bright presence will be evident in everything through Jesus, and he'll get all the credit as the One mighty in everything – encores to the end of time. Oh, yes!

1 Peter 4:1-11 (THE MESSAGE)

As we learn to think like Jesus, we see that His suffering and death provided the way to new life, a life of real purpose. From the above passage, observe how you can think like Jesus, and then describe at least three additional steps you can take to experience God's purpose for your life. _____

_____

_____

_____

_____

_____

_____

_____

_____

_____

_____

_____

_____

_____

3. Day Three: **Avoiding Disruptions to a Life of Purpose**

If you focus on past or present hurts or injustices, you cannot live in the marvelous purpose for which God has designed you. Those who focus on being merely "survivors" of sexual abuse can be stuck in the past rather than enjoying the here-and-now. It is vital for you to choose to see yourself as a person who thrives, one who can now flourish, having clear direction and hope.

Never try to be like someone else, because God has an original purpose for your life. Consider the following by Myles Munroe: "In new birth, God reclaims what is rightfully His. He redirects the natural skills and abilities that Satan perverted and employs them for the completion of His plans and purposes. Taking away what is destroying you, He encourages you to rediscover all those things that you like to do. As He restores His anointing on your life, the power to perform with excellence reinstates the beauty and the perfection of your innate abilities."[95]

As you've worked through this "journey of hope," what are some ways you see God restoring your life and working in and through you? _____

_____

_____

_____

_____

_____

_____

There will always be circumstances, people and challenges to face. You can face them in God's strength, allowing Him to restore and rebuild your core. Consider a prayer of King David that helped him stay on track.

 Explore - *Listen and help, O God. I'm reduced to a whine and a whimper, obsessed with feelings of doomsday. Don't let them find me — the conspirators out to get me, using their tongues as weapons, flinging poison words, poison-tipped arrow-words. They shoot from ambush, shoot without warning, not caring who they hit. They keep fit doing calisthenics of evil purpose, they keep lists of the traps they've secretly set. They say to each other, "No one can catch us, no one can detect our perfect crime." The Detective detects the mystery in the dark of the cellar heart. The God of the Arrow shoots! They double up in pain, fall flat on their faces in full view of the grinning crowd. Everyone sees it. God's work is the talk of the town. Be glad, good people! Fly to God! Good-hearted people, make praise your habit.*

Psalm 64, THE MESSAGE

King David acknowledged his feelings; he did not ignore the trauma in his life. He entrusted his fears, others' cruelty and evil, and his pain to God. He exchanged his suffering for God's relief. Instead of living in terror, he lived in praise, confident that God would keep him safe.

> ℬ ℭ
>
> Everyone has his own specific vocation or mission in life; everyone must carry out a concrete assignment that demands fulfillment. Therein he cannot be replaced, nor can his life be repeated, thus, everyone's task is unique as his specific opportunity to implement it.[96]
>
> Viktor E. Frankl
>
> ℬ ℭ

How will you entrust your fears and difficulties to God? _____

_____

_____

_____

Even after we give our lives to God, there are continual distractions to a consistent focus on Him. James 4:13-15 (NASU) explains the difference between an eternal focus and one that is earthly and fleeting. *Come now, you who say, "Today or tomorrow we will go to such and such a city, and spend a year there and engage in business and make a profit.' Yet you do not know what your life will be like tomorrow. You are just a vapor that appears for a little while and then vanishes away. Instead, you ought to say, 'If the Lord wills, we will live and also do this or that."*

Some common distractions to a God-focused life are represented by the CHAFF Chart below. In nature, chaff is the protective husk around a kernel of grain such as wheat; chaff is removed during threshing. Chaff serves a purpose during the plant's time of growth, but it is not useful after the plant has matured. The Bible describes chaff as something "blown by the wind, like smoke from a chimney" (Hosea 13:3, NLT), and what one day will "burn up...with fire" (Luke 3:17, NIV).

The CHAFF Chart helps you to understand that *Circumstances, Health, Appearance, Family or Friends* and/or *Finances* can all be chaff. Though each element in the chart is a useful part of life; it is not worthy of being your life's purpose. The chart provides a place to write down the times you rely on any form of CHAFF instead of on God. Through God's grace and power, you can learn to live in His provision instead of the world's temporary satisfaction. Ask God to search your heart, thanking Him that He can use CHAFF as a vehicle of growth in your life, then write down recent times you have depended on CHAFF rather than God for peace, hope, purpose, joy, or comfort. (A full-page chart is available for you to copy in Appendix C.)

Circumstances	
Health	
Appearance	
Family or Friends	
Finances	

In nature, chaff is the protective husk around a kernel of grain such as wheat; the chaff is removed during threshing. Though chaff serves a purpose during the plant's time of growth, it is not useful after the plant has developed.

ᔥ ᔥ

4. Day Four: **You Are More Than a Conqueror!**

Numerous promises in Romans 8:31-39 offer help for living consistently with hope and purpose. The passage is divided into sections below, to help you consider specific ways to live not merely as a survivor of sexual abuse but as someone who thrives—literally, as "more than a conqueror"!

As you read each of the following verses, record your observations; state what the verse means to you; and how you can apply it as you consider your life's purpose.

31 *What then shall we say to [all] this? If God is for us, who [can be] against us? [Who can be our foe, if God is on our side?]*

____

____

____

32 *He who did not withhold or spare [even] His own Son but gave Him up for us all, will He not also with Him freely and graciously give us all [other] things?*

____

____

____

33 *Who shall bring any charge against God's elect [when it is] God Who justifies [that is, Who puts us in right relation to Himself? Who shall come forward and accuse or impeach those whom God has chosen? Will God, Who acquits us?]*

____

____

____

34 *Who is there to condemn [us]? Will Christ Jesus (the Messiah), Who died, or rather Who was raised from the dead, Who is at the right hand of God actually pleading as He intercedes for us?*

____

____

____

35 *Who shall ever separate us from Christ's love? Shall suffering and affliction and tribulation? Or calamity and distress? Or persecution or hunger or destitution or peril or sword?*

____

____

____

We've been made more than conquerors, overcomers in this life.
We've been made victorious through the blood of Jesus Christ!
When troubles come knockin' at your door,
don't be afraid,
you know it's not like before.
Don't you give in,
don't let it bring you down.
Cause you don't have to worry anymore! [97]

Acappella *(Lyrics)*

^{36}*Even as it is written, For Thy sake we are put to death all the day long; we are regarded and counted as sheep for the slaughter.*

---

^{37}*Yet amid all these things we are more than conquerors and gain a surpassing victory through Him Who loved us.*

---

^{38}*For I am persuaded beyond doubt (am sure) that neither death nor life, nor angels nor principalities, nor things impending and threatening nor things to come, nor powers,*

---

^{39}*Nor height nor depth, nor anything else in all creation will be able to separate us from the love of God which is in Christ Jesus our Lord.*

ഇ ൬

You are more than a conqueror because of Jesus' death and resurrection. Because He died and rose again, you are free to live in and through His power.

ഇ ൬

You are more than a conqueror because of Jesus' death and resurrection. Because He died and rose again, you are free to live in and through His power. You need to remember that, until Jesus calls you home, you are living in a state of warfare. Thankfully, God provided everything you need for each battle you will face. Ephesians 6 describes the armor supplied for your protection and gives practical ideas for living in a state of mental and spiritual preparation for victory.

 Explore - *Finally, be strong in the Lord and in his mighty power. Put on the full armor of God so that you can take your stand against the devil's schemes. For our struggle is not against flesh and blood, but against the rulers, against the authorities, against the powers of this dark world and against the spiritual forces of evil in the heavenly realms. Therefore put on the full armor of God, so that when the day of evil comes, you may be able to stand your ground, and after you have done everything, to stand. Stand firm then, with the belt of truth buckled around your waist, with the breastplate of righteousness in place, and with your feet fitted with the readiness that comes from the gospel of peace. In addition to all this, take up the shield of faith, with which you can extinguish all the flaming arrows of the evil one. Take the helmet of salvation and the sword of the Spirit, which is the word of God. And pray in the Spirit on all occasions*

with all kinds of prayers and requests. With this in mind, be alert and always keep on praying for all the saints.

Ephesians 6:10-18, NIV

Reflect on this passage from Ephesians and answer the following questions about the armor God has provided...**and remember to put on every piece of your armor every day!**

Why do you need to put on the **full** armor of God? _____
_____
_____

Against whom are you struggling? _____
_____

What is the purpose of each of the following pieces of armor? (Note: as Paul was writing the letter to the Ephesians, he was in prison, always in the presence of a Roman centurion, acutely aware of each item listed.)

The belt of truth: _____
_____

The breastplate of righteousness: _____
_____

Feet fitted with the gospel of peace: _____
_____

The shield of faith: _____
_____

The helmet of salvation: _____
_____

The sword of the Spirit which is the Word of God (your only offensive weapon):
_____
_____

Why does Paul end this section with the reminder to be alert and always keep on praying? _____
_____
_____
_____

80 CB

These verses are not a picture of how to fight, but of how not to fight. If you have **not** put on the armor, you will have to fight; but "having put on the whole armor of God, then stand" says Paul. There are times when God's servants are sent out to attack ...but the counsel given here is as to how we are to hold the position which has been gained. [98]

Oswald Chambers

80 CB

5. Day Five: **Your Personal Vision Statement**

As you prepare to write a personal vision statement, you need to develop a clear focus. Pray and ask God to give you wisdom and direction before you proceed. Remember, God created you with a purpose and with good works to accomplish (see Ephesians 2:10). Begin thinking about your vision statement, using the following verses from Proverbs as a compass.

Trust in the Lord with all your heart, and lean not on your own understanding; in all your ways acknowledge Him, and He shall direct your paths. Proverbs 3:5-6, NKJV

We can make our plans, but the Lord determines our steps. Proverbs 16:9, NLT

Your personal vision statement, written in one or two sentences, can become a guide for your life—it describes where you are going. As you trust God and seek Him, He provides the direction necessary to guide the course of your days and the choices you will make about life.

The following are things to consider before you write your vision statement.

What excites me? _____
_____
_____
_____

What gets me up in the morning? _____
_____
_____
_____

Am I enjoying what I'm doing? Am I having fun doing it? _____
_____
_____
_____

The following things fill my tank: _____
_____
_____
_____

The following things drain my tank: _____
_____
_____
_____

ৰ০ ৫৪

Be Thou my Vision, O Lord of my heart; Naught be all else to me, save that Thou art. Thou my best Thought, by day or by night, Waking or sleeping, Thy presence my light. [99]

Be Thou My Vision
Irish hymn from the 8th century translated by Mary E. Bryne

ৰ০ ৫৪

Complete the following statements:

Eventually, I _____
_____
_____

I enjoy _____
_____

My education has _____
_____
_____

Based on my experience _____
_____
_____

I expect to _____
_____

I am equipped to _____
_____

I am exhausted by _____
_____

I am energized by _____
_____

Emotionally, I _____
_____

Some people like to combine a personal vision statement (where they're going) with a personal mission statement (a description of why they exist). Following are two examples of vision statements (the first begins with a mission statement in the first sentence and vision statement in the second).

Sue's mission and vision statements: "I want to know Christ and make Him known by investing my life serving Him with all my heart, mind, soul and strength. For the next year, that means teaching kindergarteners with passion and enthusiasm, demonstrating God's love in my classroom."

Matt's vision statement: "I am equipped to help children suffering from AIDs and am committed to wholeheartedly serve God by helping children in Rwanda whose lives have been devastated by AIDs."

Review everything that you noted about your passions, and begin to write one or two sentences that will be your personal vision statement (where you're going) for the next six months. Your life is dynamic. As you walk by faith, trusting God to use you to accomplish your vision statement, you may see Him redirecting you from time to time. When you see you are being redirected, review the Proverbs at the beginning of this section for clarity and renewed vision.

Now, write down your vision statement (extra space is provided for you to write changes as needed): _____

_____

_____

_____

_____

_____

_____

_____

_____

_____

_____

_____

_____

_____

_____

_____

_____

_____

80 03

I have strength for all things in Christ Who empowers me [I am ready for anything and equal to anything through Him Who infuses inner strength into me; I am self-sufficient in Christ's sufficiency].

Philippians 4:13, AMP

80 03

Week Nine - Weekend Bonus Work

The seventh stage of psychosocial development is Early Adulthood, from ages 24 through 34. The central process of development in this stage is mutuality among peers.[101] Early Adulthood is an important time to understand belonging.

If you don't have close relationships, a sense of isolation can occur. The developmental disruption delivered by sexual abuse during this or an earlier developmental stage can fuel an unhealthy dependence on others, with a survivor insisting each friendship be exclusive, demanding a friend's sole attention and not allowing him or her to develop other friendships.

To avoid an unhealthy dependence on others, you can develop new interests and learn to enjoy living in each moment, wherever you are in life.

Describe one or two new interests you could develop. _____

_____

_____

_____

During Early Adulthood, developmental tasks include experiencing intimate relationships, having children, and/or working, either at home or outside the home. Wherever you are, it is important to allow yourself to enjoy who you are created to be, becoming conscious of God's presence.

Throughout Early Adulthood, Luke struggled with intimacy in his marriage.

"Actually, my wife struggled more than I did," he says now. "I had little interest in sex, though I deeply loved my wife. She thought I didn't find her attractive, but I did. I think what helped us survive those difficult years was applying 1 Corinthians 7:3-5. We had intimate relations, even though my unconscious negative attitude kept me from abandoning myself to enjoy lovemaking with my wife.

It wasn't until after this developmental stage—I was almost 40—when I remembered having been sexually abused at age 5. I had suppressed that traumatic memory for nearly 35 years! When I remembered a group of boys sexually molesting me on the way home from school, I realized why I couldn't enjoy intimacy with my wife. That one incident made everything about my sexuality seem dirty and bad, all because of what those boys did to me.

During the years I wasn't sexually "engaged," my wife prayed that God would give us joyful intimacy. God answered her prayers. After I remembered and healed from my abuse, my wife and I began to experience incredible fulfillment in marital intimacy. In addition, medical tests revealed I had low testosterone levels. My doctor prescribed a supplement that increases my testosterone level, which also helps in the area of intimacy."

How does Luke's story encourage you? _____

_____

_____

_____

_____

_____

_____

_____

_____

_____

_____

_____

But he said to me, "My grace is sufficient for you, for my power is made perfect in weakness." Therefore I will boast all the more gladly about my weaknesses, so that Christ's power may rest on me. That is why, for Christ's sake, I delight in weaknesses, in insults, in hardships, in persecutions, in difficulties. For when I am weak, then I am strong.

2 Corinthians 12:9-10, NIV

Seeking to belong is a universal desire. People identify themselves as *belonging* in specific cultures or countries; as being from states, provinces or territories within their countries. We introduce ourselves as being from cities, towns, or villages within various regions, or as having grown up in a particular location.

Whether it's a book club whose members share insights about a specific book; an international group focusing on global awareness; a dance troupe known for its interpretive flair; a church or a family; belonging means acceptance, relationship, shared interests and camaraderie. Every culture exhibits specialization in its music, foods, dance, worship and traditions. These unique characteristics in diverse cultures help members feel a sense of being part of something that matters. Not surprisingly, social media sites like Facebook can fuel a sense of not belonging, particularly when you notice others with hundreds of Facebook "friends" or thousands of "followers" on Twitter.

For people of faith, identifying with a group of believers is an important part of belonging. In healthy churches, as in healthy families, members share significant aspects of life with others who understand and care about their values, hopes, problems, joys and sorrows. The sense of being part of something is damaged by all forms of abuse, whether sexual, emotional, physical, mental or spiritual. Many who experience spiritual abuse in church say it feels like emotional rape.

The incredible psychosocial disruption of sexual abuse can shatter the core sense of belonging. At any age, sexual exploitation delivers varying levels of anxiety, fear, revulsion, depression, or despair. Not knowing who is safe to trust or where one belongs erodes the foundation needed for building relationships. This chapter will help you know how to belong, and where to be safe.

Core Healing Goal: to understand and identify where you belong.

1. Day One: **Belonging in Church**

   Sadly, churches are frequently a place where individuals feel ostracized if they are different in any way. In the United States, for example, the racism of the 1960s left millions traumatized in churches that disrespected and devalued an entire group of people created in the image of God.

   In twenty-first century churches throughout the world, marginalization and minimalization of people continues, in many forms. Those who don't have homes or clean clothing might experience one form of minimalization; those with ideas different from a church's focus are marginalized in other ways.

> The sense of being part of something is damaged when there is any form of abuse, whether sexual, emotional, physical, mental or spiritual.

There is profound confusion in a survivor of sexual abuse who believes s/he doesn't fit in with people at church. If survivors are told—either directly or indirectly that they are "damaged goods," it is almost impossible for them to feel safe at church. Further damage occurs if there is manipulation, rejection, blame, subtle coercion, or other forms of abuse in church, a place where people should experience safety and protection. [Note: if you are currently being abused in church, ask God to lead you to a safe church.]

God created people with innate worth. Every person was designed to be loved, respected and valued. If you do not feel valued in your church, speak up (if possible) to promote positive change.

William Wilberforce recognized appalling abuse—slavery—in Great Britain two centuries ago; for over eighteen years, he used his position of influence to persistently introduce anti-slavery motions in Parliament. Though repeatedly discouraged, Wilberforce persevered until the slave trade was finally abolished in Great Britain in 1807. Even so, the evil persisted in the British colonies. In "Amazing Grace," Eric Metaxas wrote about that struggle, observing "The morning after abolition's victory, 500,000 human beings remained imprisoned as slaves." And slavery persisted in British colonies until 1833.[102]

If you are discouraged about the ongoing ramifications of sexual abuse, ask God if He wants you to speak up or help in other ways. One important thing we all can do is pray for people wounded by sexual abuse. We can stop ignoring hurtful ways people treat each other at church and elsewhere, applying what Jesus tells us in Luke 6:31, *"Do to others as you would have them do to you."*

In "Soul Survivor," Philip Yancey wrote about his struggles regarding behavior in church. "Sometimes in a waiting room or on an airplane I strike up conversations with strangers, during the course of which they learn that I write books on spiritual themes. Eyebrows arch, barriers spring up, and often I hear yet another horror story about church. My seatmates must expect me to defend the church, because they always act surprised when I respond, 'Oh, it's even worse than that. Let me tell you my story.'"[103]

Yancey continued, "Though I had emerged from childhood churches badly damaged, as I began to scrutinize Jesus through the critical eyes of a journalist, I saw that the qualities that so upset me—legalism, self-righteousness, racism, provincialism, hypocrisy—Jesus had fought against, and were probably the very qualities that led to his crucifixion. Getting to know the God revealed in Jesus, I recognized I needed to change in many ways—yes, even to repent, for I had absorbed the hypocrisy, racism, and self-righteousness of my upbringing and contributed numerous sins of my own. I began to envision God less as a stern judge shaking his finger at my waywardness than as a doctor who prescribes behavior in my best interest in order to safeguard my health."[104]

80 03

The most insidious, divisive, and wounding power is the power used in the service of God.[105]

Henri Nouwen

80 03

130

In what ways can you look at God as a physician who prescribes behavior, relationships, and new ways of thinking that can safeguard your physical, mental, emotional and spiritual health"? _____

_____

_____

_____

You cannot rely on people to tell you whether you belong; you can rely on Jesus. He never changes; He will never fail you. Jeremiah explained one reason people disappoint each other.

The heart is deceitful above all things and beyond cure. Who can understand it? He answered His own question in the next verse: *I the Lord search the heart and examine the mind, to reward a man according to his conduct, according to what his deeds deserve.* Jeremiah 17:9-10, NIV

Since the fall of man, the human heart has had the potential for evil. Knowing that and realizing that people lie to one another, gossip about each other, or hurt one another in various ways, can we really be surprised that hurtful things happen in churches, where groups of people gather? Instead, we can have a realistic awareness that church is a place where broken people go to find hope and healing. Then we aren't disappointed when we realize that even people at church cannot meet our innermost needs.

Jeremiah addresses the root issue regarding why people hurt each other. *For My people have committed two evils: they have forsaken Me, the fountain of living waters, to hew for themselves cisterns, broken cisterns that can hold no water* (Jeremiah 2:13, NASU).

Our human tendency is to worship anyone or anything but God. John Calvin described the human heart as an "idol factory." Jeremiah indicated we easily drift toward "broken cisterns that can hold no water." In other words, we try to find peace, hope, joy, love and life in people, circumstances, substances, things or activities rather than in God. And God alone can fill us with living water; He alone truly satisfies. If you wonder whether you are worshipping God or something or someone else, simply observe where you turn when you need comfort. Often who or what we turn to for comfort is what we are worshipping. Only God will never fail.

In John 4:10, Jesus offers living water to you. Not only will He provide for your core need to belong; He provides His Holy Spirit to give you hope regardless of your circumstances. Will you allow the Holy Spirit to give you hope where you are right now? ____ Yes ____ No Explain. _____

_____

_____

_____

_____

ഇ ര

Since the fall of man, the human heart has had the potential for evil. Knowing that and realizing that people lie to one another, gossip about each other, or hurt one another in various ways, can we really be surprised that hurtful things happen in churches, where groups of people gather?

ഇ ര

In his book, "Practicing the Presence of People," Mike Mason describes the one message his friend Bob Kirk, a pastor, wishes he could convey to people in church, especially to leaders. Kirk said, "I'd like to tell the church to let people be human. I'd like them to learn to enjoy humanity, both their own and others.' To enjoy and to accept humanity, with all its warts and weaknesses, without pulling away in fear and judgment—this is the one thing the church doesn't know. Most churches, I think, are frightened of human beings."[106]

If people have pulled away from you, it could be because they either do not understand the core damage of sexual abuse or are afraid of their own inadequacy to help.

 Explore - On the last and greatest day of the Feast, Jesus stood and said in a loud voice, "If anyone is thirsty, let him come to me and drink. Whoever believes in me, as the Scripture has said, streams of living water will flow from within him." By this he meant the Spirit, whom those who believed in him were later to receive. Up to that time the Spirit had not been given, since Jesus had not yet been glorified.

John 7:37-39, NIV

Neither your emotions nor other people are accurate indicators of reality. Both can mislead you. Instead of entrusting yourself to flawed guides to help you find a place where you can belong, will you entrust yourself to God? ____ Yes ____ No How? _____

_____

_____

_____

_____

What activities, attitudes or actions have you relied on to give you a sense of belonging? _____

_____

_____

_____

_____

As you read Romans 15:5-7, think about God's acceptance and how it can impact the way people in a church behave toward one another.

May the God who gives endurance and encouragement give you a spirit of unity among yourselves as you follow Christ Jesus, so that with one heart and mouth you may glorify the God and Father of our Lord Jesus Christ. Accept one another, then, just as Christ accepted you, in order to bring praise to God.

ℰℭ ℭℬ

In a world awash with insecurity and in search of acceptance, we need biblical anchors to hold on to.[107]

Gary Smalley & John Trent

ℰℭ ℭℬ

Your potential to belong is not based on how people treat you but on the fact that God sent Jesus for you. God Himself accepts you! When Christians accept each other, it results in praise to God. How does an attitude of praising God transform our communication with each other?

_____

_____

_____

_____

In what specific ways will you entrust yourself to your loving God rather than putting your hope in people? _____

_____

_____

_____

2. Day Two: **Fitting In**

A common challenge for survivors of sexual abuse is the strong belief that they will never "fit in" with normal people. Keep in mind that "normal" is a relative word—as Patsy Clairmont said, "Normal is just a setting on your dryer."[108] If you are trying to belong with so-called normal people, you might never find a group of truly safe people. You can begin the process by choosing to believe you are just as worthy as anyone else. Secondly, you can look for a place where you can serve others rather than waiting for someone to notice you. Having a godly self-respect will help you know what groups are right for you.

At the same time, it is important to be aware of any attitudes or actions you need to change in order to improve how you relate with others. Check any of the following harmful behaviors or attitudes that currently apply to you:

❑ Negativity—a critical attitude about circumstances, events and people
❑ Lying—in any of its forms
❑ Sarcasm—using humor that directly or indirectly wounds, criticizes or mocks others
❑ Gossip—giving information about someone else to anyone who is not part of the situation, concern, or its solution
❑ Slander—spreading false information that damages another person's reputation
❑ Manipulating and/or misleading others
❑ Doing for others what they can do for themselves
❑ Being consistently late for appointments
❑ Passive-aggression (holding on to anger, resentment, or frustration

toward others; instead of honestly addressing and working through interpersonal conflict, expressing it passively with stubbornness, criticism, procrastination, withholding affection, etc.)

❑ Blaming—demanding others assume responsibility for your current suffering rather than assuming responsibility for your own change and growth

❑ Poor impulse control (reacting instead of responding)

❑ Arrogance or self-deprecation (focusing on yourself, with either an attitude of pride or self-criticism)

❑ Jealousy—believing others have more than you do and desiring what they have; not being grateful for what you have

❑ Talking "over" people; not listening when others are speaking

❑ Believing your opinions, talents or achievements matter more than others' opinions, talents or achievements [everyone wants to be respected, valued and appreciated]

❑ Believing your opinions, talents or achievements matter less than others' opinions, talents or achievements [if you are rejecting yourself, your attitude will rub off on others]

❑ Imposing what you want on others; taking control

❑ Talking about your problems or concerns in most "conversations" [if you don't know if you do this, stop yourself the next time you are with someone and notice whether you let the other person talk about his or her concerns—and if you listen to what he or she says]

❑ Not caring about others' needs

❑ Bullying—using intimidation, blame or threats to get your way

❑ Jumping to conclusions about what others are thinking rather than seeking to understand them

❑ Not keeping commitments

Please don't be discouraged if a number of the behaviors and attitudes listed currently apply to you. Look at this as a wonderful opportunity to allow God to fill your life with fresh insight and new growth. As you spend time in His Word every day, you can find limitless practical ideas to apply in your relationships.

To continue your growth process, write out 1 Corinthians 13:4-8.

_____

_____

_____

_____

_____

_____

_____

_____

_____

_____

ॐ ﷼

When you as a Christian consider the fact that your life was formed from its beginning by Jesus Christ and that He continues to shape you into His own image, then you can begin to feel good about yourself.[110]

Dick Wulf

ॐ ﷼

Describe several qualities you see in 1 Corinthians 13 that can help you improve how you relate with others. _____

_____

_____

_____

_____

_____

 Explore - Colossians 3:12-17 (NASU) offers additional ideas for change and growth. *So, as those who have been chosen of God, holy and beloved, put on a heart of compassion, kindness, humility, gentleness and patience; bearing with one another, and forgiving each other, whoever has a complaint against anyone; just as the Lord forgave you, so also should you. Beyond all these things put on love, which is the perfect bond of unity. Let the peace of Christ rule in your hearts, to which indeed you were called in one body; and be thankful. Let the word of Christ richly dwell within you, with all wisdom teaching and admonishing one another with psalms and hymns and spiritual songs, singing with thankfulness in your hearts to God. Whatever you do in word or deed, do all in the name of the Lord Jesus, giving thanks through Him to God the Father.*

What statements in Colossians 3:12-17 help you understand God's love for you? _____

_____

_____

_____

_____

_____

_____

_____

_____

_____

Will you ask God to help you show His love to others? ____ Yes ____ No Why? _____

_____

In Colossians 3:12-17, what specific positive attitudes and actions do you notice that you can apply in your relationships? _____

_____

_____

_____

_____

_____

ဆ ca

Jesus' acceptance of people is not based on ignorance of them and their circumstance. This fact should speak powerfully to people with avoidant personalities who believe that if people knew what they were really like, they would reject them. Time and time again we find people commenting on how Jesus seemed to see right to the heart of their very being.[111]

Joanna McGrath and Alister McGrath

ဆ ca

When you have time, read through both 1 and 2 Samuel and the Psalms; there you'll see that there were many times King David didn't fit in. He hurt people and was hurt by them, yet God referred to him as "a man after His own heart" (1 Samuel 13:14, NASU). David expressed his feelings to God: *When my spirit was overwhelmed within me, then You knew my path. In the way in which I walk they have secretly set a snare for me. Look on my right hand and see, for there is no one who acknowledges me; refuge has failed me; no one cares for my soul. I cried out to You, O Lord: I said, "You are my refuge, my portion in the land of the living."* Psalm 142:3-5, NKJV

At any time, anywhere, you can cry out to God, telling Him exactly how you feel. He cares; He wants to comfort you and be your safe haven. Read David's entire prayer in Psalm 142; in response, write a prayer communicating your concerns. _____

_____

_____

_____

_____

_____

_____

3. Day Three: **The Battle to Forgive in the Battle to Belong**

Chapters Five and Six provided an in-depth look at forgiveness. As we consider the core concern of belonging, it is important to review the essence of forgiveness.

Dr. Dan B. Allender and Dr. Tremper Longman III state, "One reason we are so easily blinded to the vital importance of forgiveness is our penchant to deny that we are in a war. The Evil One wants us to question God. He desires, even more, for us to ignore the need to grapple with God or the world in which we live. *We will see the importance of forgiveness as a central category in relating to others to the extent that we see every relationship enmeshed in a war that leads to a taste of heaven or hell.* If we understand the battle we are engaged in and the nature of the wounds we experience, forgiveness is seen as the foundation for comprehending the goodness of God and the only hope for restored relationships with others."[112]

In what ways do relationships demonstrate a taste of either heaven or hell?

_____

_____

_____

_____

I cry out loudly to God, loudly I plead with God for mercy. I spill out all my complaints before him, and spell out my troubles in detail:

Psalm 142:1-2, *THE MESSAGE*

Psalm 32 provides a look at the forgiveness and restoration available to each of us. Relating effectively with others begins with a right relationship with God; with an accurate understanding of His love and provision for our core need to belong.

 Explore - *BLESSED (HAPPY, fortunate, to be envied) is he who has forgiveness of his transgression continually exercised upon him, whose sin is covered. Blessed (happy, fortunate, to be envied) is the man to whom the Lord imputes no iniquity and in whose spirit there is no deceit. When I kept silence [before I confessed], my bones wasted away through my groaning all the day long. For day and night Your hand [of displeasure] was heavy upon me; my moisture was turned into the drought of summer. Selah [pause, and calmly think of that]! I acknowledged my sin to You, and my iniquity I did not hide. I said, I will confess my transgressions to the Lord [continually unfolding the past till all is told] — then You [instantly] forgave me the guilt and iniquity of my sin. Selah [pause, and calmly think of that]! For this [forgiveness] let everyone who is godly pray — pray to You in a time when You may be found; surely when the great waters [of trial] overflow, they shall not reach [the spirit in] him. You are a hiding place for me; You, Lord, preserve me from trouble, You surround me with songs and shouts of deliverance. Selah [pause, and calmly think of that]! I [the Lord] will instruct you and teach you in the way you should go; I will counsel you with My eye upon you. Be not like the horse or the mule, which lack understanding, which must have their mouths held firm with bit and bridle, or else they will not come with you. Many are the sorrows of the wicked, but he who trusts in, relies on, and confidently leans on the Lord shall be compassed about with mercy and with loving-kindness. Be glad in the Lord and rejoice, you [uncompromisingly] righteous [you who are upright and in right standing with Him]; shout for joy, all you upright in heart! Psalm 32, AMP.*

Psalm 32:1 states that forgiveness results in being "blessed (HAPPY, fortunate, to be envied)." That theme continues in verse two. Before we can be in healthy relationships with others, we need to allow God to cleanse us from our sins. Have you done that? ____ Yes ____ No Explain. _____

_____

_____

_____

_____

Psalm 32:7 describes God as "a hiding place." In verse 8, the Lord says He "will instruct you and teach you in the way you should go [and] counsel you with [His] eye upon you." Will you allow Him to lead and teach you, and to provide a safe place for you amidst the sorrows of the world? ____ Yes ____ No Explain. _____

_____

_____

_____

As we consider how God redeems and recycles the negative and painful events of our lives, we need to consider also the somewhat obvious fact that He redeems the positive events as well.[113]

Dick Wulf

Jesus understands the challenges you face. He said, *I've told you all this so that trusting me, you will be unshakable and assured, deeply at peace. In this godless world you will continue to experience difficulties. But take heart! I've conquered the world.* John 16:33 (THE MESSAGE).

You can experience belonging, in God's unfailing love. After you think about Psalm 32 and John 16:33, write out a prayer of response to God. Prayer is simply talking with God; do not worry about getting the words "right;" the Lover of your soul loves to hear from you. _____

_____

_____

_____

_____

_____

_____

_____

_____

_____

_____

_____

_____

_____

_____

_____

4. Day Four: **To Trust or Not to Trust**

If you didn't have a loving father, if your father molested you, or if a stepfather or other father-figure abused you in any way, the concept of belonging may push you to despair. If your mother or another female molested you, it could be extremely difficult to believe you could feel safe belonging anywhere. Forgiveness releases you from the clutches of the past!

If there were alcoholism or other substance abuse in your family, you likely learned to live by the three unspoken rules of the addict's home: Don't Talk; Don't Trust; Don't Feel. Working through this book might be the first time you allowed yourself to notice and feel the pain of disconnection in your family-of-origin that is known as emotional cut-off. To understand how to belong, you can move beyond what *feels* normal to what *is* true.

Because sexual abusers assume power over their victims, survivors of sexual abuse often continue feeling powerless for years or decades after the molestation occurred. A relational downside of disempowerment is not knowing who to trust. Having a sense of belonging begins with being able to trust. If you have been betrayed or repeatedly hurt, you likely have some skepticism about people. Defining who you can trust takes time coupled

----

Don't Talk.

Don't Trust.

Don't Feel.

Claudia Black

138

with a determination to grow and know both the people who are safe as well as where you really want to belong.

In what ways do you need to build your ability to trust safe people? _____
_____
_____

Write down the names of one or two safe people you have met during your life, noting the qualities that made them safe for you to know. (If you have never felt safe with anyone, look for two safe people in the Bible and describe them here.) _____
_____
_____

Read the entire Gospel of John during the next several weeks. Today, read John 17:20-26. This is Jesus' prayer for all believers. Describe what Jesus says about *how* you belong, noticing He sees all believers as one in Him. (What difference can the reality of belonging in Christ make in your perception of your worth in His family?) _____
_____
_____
_____
_____
_____
_____
_____

ဆ ၹ

If I have a distorted view of the past, the present, God, the future, and myself, there is no way I will respond properly to what God has allowed in my life.[114]

Paul David Tripp

ဆ ၹ

5. Day Five: **Belonging by Being**

As you make new choices, you can discover the simple joy of living in the moment—as the human being God created you to be. God Himself built you to belong. Rather than blaming your past for your current concerns, allow yourself to live in today, consciously creating a different world for yourself and the people in your life. Just as a house is built board-by-board or brick-by-brick, you can build proactively as you relate with others. Your choice to think creatively can help you make the step-by-step positive choices that are essential to building healthy relationships.

In our self-centered world, many people feel lonely. When individuals have been hurt over and over, they might refer to themselves as "losers" or "misfits." Instead of giving yourself negative labels, train yourself to focus on

God's love and acceptance. Giving yourself negative labels keeps you trapped; becoming the person God created you to be frees you to live.

Notice and write down any negative labels you give yourself. Pay attention to negative automatic thoughts, such as "I'll never fit in. I don't belong anywhere. I'm a failure." _____

_____

_____

_____

Write down positive descriptions to replace past or current negative labels you have accepted about yourself, e.g. "I am now accepted in Christ forever. I'll always belong in His love." Remember to use Truth as positive self-talk to replace negative self-talk each time it occurs. _____

_____

_____

_____

An important aspect of learning to belong is learning to care about others, noticing their needs and concerns. People who are uncaring, unkind or cruel frequently have one of two problems: either they are arrogant and egotistical or they are insecure. Either condition is self-centered, which can keep people stuck in unhealthy behavior. Instead, you can be secure—and sincere in caring about others, helping them belong and caring about their needs as well as your own.

In psychology, one characteristic of a healthy self-perspective is referred to as having an "internal locus of control." With an internal locus of control, you are aware that you can make beneficial core choices regardless of where you are or what is happening. Since you are not defined by either external circumstances or by people, you do not live as a victim but as a creator. You live in the present moment rather than the past. You choose to trust in God to give you peace in the moment and strength to face every concern.

For a Christian, Christ is the locus of control; the central focus. The apostle Paul explained, "I have been crucified with Christ; it is no longer I who live, but Christ lives in me; and the life which I now live in the flesh I live by faith in the Son of God, who loved me and gave Himself for me" (Galatians 2:20, NKJV).

How would relying on Christ as your locus of control help you discover a sense of belonging? _____

_____

_____

   ℰ   ℭ

Hypocrisy is the essence of snobbery, but all snobbery is about the problem of belonging.[115]

Alexander Theroux

   ℰ   ℭ

In His strength, you can apply Jesus' command to *"Love your neighbor as yourself."* Notice the statement Jesus made before He explained how to love others. Asked by religious leaders, *"'Teacher, which is the greatest commandment in the Law?' Jesus replied: 'Love the Lord your God with all your heart and with all your soul and with all your mind.' This is the first and greatest commandment. And the second is like it: 'Love your neighbor as yourself.'"* Matthew 22:36-39, NIV

Mike Mason wrote, "Jesus' second great commandment implies that we will love others only to the extent that we love ourselves. The command might be better understood by putting the words 'You will' in front of it: *'You will love your neighbor as yourself.'* That is, the feelings you have toward yourself will inevitably be projected upon others. If you do not love yourself, you will not love your neighbor. If you are not real to yourself, no one else will be real to you either."[116]

 Explore - *Blessed be the God and Father of our Lord Jesus Christ, who has blessed us with every spiritual blessing in the heavenly places in Christ, just as He chose us in Him before the foundation of the world, that we would be holy and blameless before Him. In love He predestined us to adoption as sons through Jesus Christ to Himself, according to the kind intention of His will, to the praise of the glory of His grace, which He freely bestowed on us in the Beloved.*

Ephesians 1:3-6, NASU

Do you love yourself? _____ Yes _____ No Explain. _____
_____
_____

Think about Ephesians 1:3-6, then describe how you can live authentically in God's love, realizing He has adopted you into His family, to live freely in His unfailing love forever. _____
_____
_____
_____
_____
_____
_____
_____

As I think about adoption, I remember our granddaughter Isabelle's adoption ceremony, where the judge asked our daughter and son-in-law if they would freely give her all legal rights of being their child. Becoming God's child by being adopted into His family entitles each of us to all of the amazing privileges of being children of the King of Kings!

The psalmist said to *Delight yourself in the Lord; and He will give you the desires of your heart.* Psalm 37:4, NASU

Have you ever simply asked God to show you *what to want?* You won't want something or someone harmful when you fully rely on God to lead you. He loves you; He cares about you; He wants to provide for your needs. Think about what you enjoy doing and write about a place where you could meet people of similar interests. _____

_____

_____

_____

_____

If you have failed in the past, you can choose to enjoy the present and look forward to the future. Zig Ziglar explains, "Failure is an event, not a person. So regardless of what happens to you along the way, you must keep on going and doing the right thing in the right way. Then the event becomes a reality of a changed life."[118]

Many organizations and individuals need volunteer assistance. A few ideas are listed below. Check all of the ideas that appeal to you.

- ❑ Help parents of children with physical, mental or emotional needs
- ❑ Address and mail letters for missionaries
- ❑ Begin training to do pet therapy with your dog
- ❑ Deliver, cook or otherwise help with a program such as Meals-on-Wheels to provide meals to people who cannot cook for themselves
- ❑ Pray for others
- ❑ Help at a hospital by delivering books, flowers, etc. to patients
- ❑ Write notes to encourage people
- ❑ Read stories at a library reading program or to children in a cancer ward
- ❑ Help with unloading, sorting, delivery, etc. at a food distribution program
- ❑ Serve, clean, cook, etc. at a soup kitchen
- ❑ Teach Sunday school
- ❑ Help in a church nursery; assist with a church office or Bible study
- ❑ Make phone calls to shut-ins
- ❑ Help at an animal shelter
- ❑ Do after-school tutoring
- ❑ Become a teacher's assistant
- ❑ Lead tours at art museums
- ❑ Explain science at a nature center
- ❑ Plant flowers in your community
- ❑ Grow vegetables to share with others

ഇ ഇ

How far you go in life depends on your being tender with the young, compassionate with the aged, sympathetic with the striving, and tolerant of the weak and the strong—because someday you will have been all of these. [119]

George Washington Carver

ഇ ഇ

- ❑ Visit people in nursing homes or hospitals who have no family caring for them
- ❑ Help someone with home projects such as yard work, painting, etc.
- ❑ Teach a class in an area you enjoy (quilting, baking, foreign languages, computers, etc.)
- ❑ Help at an orphanage

The Bible uses the metaphor of the human body to explain the reality of belonging in Christ.

Just as each of us has one body with many members, and these members do not all have the same function, so in Christ we who are many form one body, and each member belongs to all the others. We have different gifts, according to the grace given us. If a man's gift is prophesying, let him use it in proportion to his faith. If it is serving, let him serve; if it is teaching, let him teach; if it is encouraging, let him encourage; if it is contributing to the needs of others, let him give generously; if it is leadership, let him govern diligently; if it is showing mercy, let him do it cheerfully. Love must be sincere. Hate what is evil; cling to what is good. Be devoted to one another in brotherly love. Honor one another above yourselves. Never be lacking in zeal, but keep your spiritual fervor, serving the Lord. Be joyful in hope, patient in affliction, faithful in prayer. Share with God's people who are in need. Practice hospitality.

Romans 12:4-13, NIV

Each of us has different gifts that can be used to build and encourage others. Appreciating your unique worth and value as part of the body of Christ can help you become willing to share your gifts with others who will benefit from them. Can you think of ways to use the gifts God has given you to "share with God's people who are in need"? _____

_____

_____

_____

Developing traditions can help increase a sense of belonging and consistency. In your family of origin, did you have special traditions? Describe some of those traditions here. _____

_____

_____

_____

_____

_____

Review the traditions you just listed and put a check by those that you enjoyed.

ᔰ ⱌ

But if we are the Body

Why aren't His arms reaching

Why aren't His hands healing

Why aren't His words teaching

And if we are the Body

Why aren't His feet going

Why is His love not showing them there is a way. [120]

Casting Crowns
If We are the Body
(Lyrics)

ᔰ ⱌ

At any stage of life, it is possible to intentionally develop enjoyable family traditions. If you don't have a relationship with your family, look for other people you can include in your tradition-building. Many people spend holidays alone and would welcome an invitation.

Decades ago, my husband and I moved to California, with our three young daughters when our youngest daughter was just two weeks old. Lonely, living far from family, we invited Japanese students to join us for a traditional Thanksgiving meal; sharing our traditions with them made the day memorable. Years later, living in Colorado, we shared Thanksgiving with new friends from the Middle East when my husband was in graduate school. We have invited people to join some of our Christmas and Easter celebrations, too, sharing the joy of our Savior's life—and resurrection.

Many people find great satisfaction in serving holiday meals at a homeless shelter; still others enjoy having their children help them prepare gift baskets for families in need. By choosing to do something proactive and positive, you can prevent both morbid introspection and the paralysis of analysis.

If you haven't had enjoyable family traditions before now, pause and think about what you would like to do for others during various holidays, birthdays, etc. and write your positive ideas below.

Birthdays _____
_____

Easter _____
_____

Thanksgiving _____
_____

Christmas _____
_____

Other _____
_____
_____

NOTE: Single people can beautifully exhibit hospitality, so please don't use not having a family as an excuse to avoid reaching out to others. Hospitality is not about having a fancy home, being a fabulous cook, or having perfect décor. It is about making people feel welcome and wanted—helping them belong. As you appreciate your own worth, you can help others feel a sense of belonging, too. One of the best antidotes to the despair of feeling like you don't belong is helping others belong.

At any stage of life, it is possible to intentionally develop enjoyable family traditions. If you don't have a relationship with your family, look for other people you can include in your tradition-building.

Gratitude is another incredible antidote to despair.   G. K. Chesterton said, "I would maintain that thanks are the highest form of thought; and that gratitude is happiness doubled by wonder."[121] As you consider your work in the five core areas—Competence, Security, Identity, Purpose and now, Belonging, think about being grateful for the growth you're experiencing. How can you exhibit gratitude today? _____

_____

_____

_____

_____

_____

_____

_____

_____

Week Ten - Weekend Bonus Work

Middle Adulthood, from ages 34 to 60, is the eighth stage of psychosocial development. During this season of life, people often manage careers, nurture an intimate relationship, expand and build new caring relationships, manage their homes and care for extended family. [122]

One ramification of sexual abuse during or prior to this stage is becoming stagnant, having little or no interest in life or in growth as a human being. Despite abuse, it is possible to continuing growing and learning throughout life. As you rely on God for strength and healing during this developmental stage, you can continue becoming the person God designed you to be.

Anita was raped during Middle Adulthood. Molested by a leader from her church; Anita felt another kind of abuse—betrayal—when friends abandoned her after learning his version of what happened. Her perpetrator denied everything, insisting that she seduced him; Anita was profoundly devastated when some of her friends believed his cunning lies rather than the truth. She left that church but clung to God. During counseling, she realized that anyone who deserted her in her time of suffering was never really a friend at all.

Anita learned to make new friends and develop new interests during her life's middle season. She said, "For months after it happened, I felt so stressed that I thought I was going to have a heart attack. Every time I remembered the molestation, I didn't want to live; I didn't feel worthy of living. Then my Christian counselor helped me realize that I could truly forgive my abuser—and the so-called friends who abandoned me. Because the abuse was devastating, she helped me see how to forgive without reconciling with my perpetrator (who never admitted what he did) or with those who believed his lies. I wanted to confront all of them but realized it would destroy me to do so. With help, I found a safe church where I could begin again."

ଽ০ ൭ଃ

... any effort we make to prevent unnecessary stress must be centered on changing our perceptions.[123]

Richard E. Ecker

ଽ০ ൭ଃ

Recalling her abuse several years after it occurred, Anita said, "Though it once felt like the worst thing that ever happened to me, I now have deeper compassion for others than I had before. And I really listen—and care— when new friends share their problems. 2 Corinthians 12: 9-10 has helped me not only survive but learn to put all my hope in God instead of in people. I belong to Him, and in Him I can enjoy life, whether people are kind to me or not."

 Explore -*But he [Jesus] said to me, "My grace is sufficient for you, for my power is made perfect in weakness." Therefore I will boast all the more gladly about my weaknesses, so that Christ's power may rest on me. That is why, for Christ's sake, I delight in weaknesses, in insults, in hardships, in persecutions, in difficulties. For when I am weak, then I am strong.*

2 Corinthians 12:9-10, NIV

How can you apply 2 Corinthians 12:9-10 to your concerns? _____

_____

_____

_____

_____

_____

_____

_____

_____

_____

_____

_____

_____

_____

_____

_____

_____

_____

_____

_____

_____

_____

_____

_____

℘ ℭ

Hold My [Jesus] hand, and walk joyously with Me through this day. Together we will savor the pleasures and endure the difficulties it brings.[124]

Sarah Young

℘ ℭ

I Am a Victor!

Chapter Eleven

Read aloud the chapter title, "I Am a Victor!" Say it several times, noticing how saying it helps you feel empowered. The fact is: you *are* a victor! Even if you don't *feel* like a victor yet, you can keep telling yourself that *fact* until you believe it, because God promises you victory through the Lord Jesus Christ (see 1 Corinthians 15:57).

Just as computer needs to be continually checked for viruses, you need a daily check-up to make sure your thoughts aren't re-infected with the debilitating ramifications of sexual abuse. Doubting God's love is an incapacitating "virus" that can derail your progress; living in awareness of His love protects you from feeling like a victim.

When you begin to doubt the love of God the Father, Son and Holy Spirit, please review your work throughout *Core Healing*. You've worked through many issues to help you see God is not like anyone who molested you. Your heavenly Father is kind, caring, loving, faithful, tender, compassionate and good. You can doubt your doubts instead of doubting God's goodness.

This chapter provides practical ideas to keep you moving forward, instead of backward toward old disabling behaviors and beliefs. It will teach you how to identify "Victim" thinking and learn to think as a "Creator," living as a victor amid life's ongoing challenges.

If you are a family member or close friend of a survivor of sexual abuse, this chapter can help you avoid the common tendency of trying to rescue someone from emotional, physical, spiritual, relational or intellectual concerns related to molestation. You can learn to be a coach instead, confident that the survivor can not only survive the abuse but thrive, learning to face challenges in the amazing limitless strength God offers.

Core Healing Goal: to understand and apply living as a Creator/Victor instead of as a Victim.

To help reach this week's goal, we are going to explore three emotionally-disabling mindsets and three emotionally-constructive mindsets. The disabling negative mindsets—Victim, Rescuer and Persecutor—were originally illustrated by Stephen B. Karpman, M.D., via the Karpman Drama Triangle. The three positive mindsets—Creator, Coach and Challenger—were developed by David Emerald in the book, "The Power of TED* (*The Empowerment Dynamic)." These tripartite mindsets fuel either an intensely negative or incredibly positive emotional infrastructure, depending on a person's moment-by-moment choices. Your life as a Creator/Victor can begin immediately; it is not contingent on what anyone else does or doesn't do; it is a uniquely personal choice.

> ℰℬ ℭ𝒮
>
> Sow a thought and you reap an action; sow an action and you reap a habit; sow a habit and you reap a character; sow a character and you reap a destiny.[125]
>
> Ralph Waldo Emerson
>
> ℰℬ ℭ𝒮

1. Day One: **The Victim Game**

The Victim Game is a destructive form of interpersonal interaction that can subtly become a lifestyle without its participants even knowing they're players. Participants in this emotional game shift in and out of its three roles, variously changing beliefs and behaviors from **Victim** to **Rescuer** or **Persecutor**.

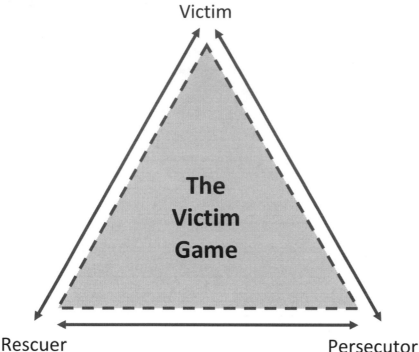

ജ ❧

You don't have to be defined by past trauma. You can move away from what happened then, consciously, persistently avoiding being derailed and disabled by the Victim Game.

ജ ❧

The role of Victim is as old as Adam and Eve; each blamed the other, and God, for their own choices. On the other hand, many people experience serious problems they have not chosen. These individuals truly have been *victimized* by other people, such as by sexual abuse; by difficult circumstances; poor health; or other serious problems they did not choose. However, not everyone who has been *victimized* chooses to live as a Victim.

Those who move into the role of **Victim** believe their status is something over which they have no control. Survivors of sexual abuse experienced the powerlessness of being controlled by someone else; therefore, many continue fearing being out of control. Your past difficulties may have been extensive and certainly were real. Therefore, it is important to differentiate between *awareness* of the difficulties of your situation or condition, and the *assumption* that you have no choice or control.

The fact is this: sexual abuse is a crime; survivors of abuse were horribly victimized in out-of-control debilitating circumstances. Learning about the emotional status of Victim does not diminish the facts of what happened; it simply helps you no longer live as someone defined by past trauma. Today, you can move away from what happened then, choosing a future of hope by consciously, determinedly seeing yourself as a Creator rather than a Victim.

How can you tell if you're living as a Victim now? Observe how you think about yourself during one day this week. If you feel persecuted, unloved, powerless, that you don't belong, or think life is happening *to* you [out of control], you may have unconsciously assumed the Victim role. David Emerald explains, "Victims may be defensive, submissive, over-accommodating to others, passive-aggressive in conflict, dependent on others for self-worth, overly sensitive, even manipulative. They're often angry, resentful, and envious, feeling unworthy or ashamed about their circumstances...every Victim has a dream that somehow has been denied or thwarted."[126] If you feel hopeless and discouraged about your present or your future, you could be in the Victim role.

In what ways do you exhibit Victim traits?_____

_____

_____

_____

_____

An important feature of the Victim Game's unwritten rules is that a person cannot declare herself/himself the Victim. Instead, the victim is anyone who has been declared Victim by someone else. A friend, family member, psychiatrist, counselor, rabbi/minister/pastor/priest, or someone else in a position of personal or public authority can confirm a person's Victim status. Many people invest significant amounts of time and money finding someone to legitimize their internal belief of Victim status. The reason for this quest is simple: individuals who admit they are living as Victims accept responsibility for being Victims, which would indicate they could actually do something about their situation, condition, experience, or problem. Recognizing responsibility is not a Victim trait.

The other two roles in the Victim Game are Rescuer and Persecutor. Recognizing the existence of Persecutors is not a form of minimizing or denying your problems; it is essential to recognize problems and to learn a new way to deal with them! In the Victim Game, though, the typical tendency is to find a Rescuer, which quickly becomes disabling rather than empowering.

A Victim, faced with a Persecutor or Persecutors, either consciously or unconsciously looks for a **Rescuer,** in the form of a person, activity or situation designated to alleviate real or perceived suffering. When a Rescuer emerges, the Victim feels a sense of empowerment, erroneously believing that the Rescuer's validation proves the validity of Victim beliefs such as, "My past suffering was so bad that I am not responsible for current difficulties in my life. My identity is defined by my problems." For individuals facing genuine difficulties, capitulating to the role of Victim reduces them from people who can choose beneficial responses to people who let their circumstances or other people compel them to *react* rather than *respond*.

A Rescuer works hard to "help" others with problems or concerns, perhaps trying to fill a void in his or her own life with the temporary satisfaction of trying to control or "fix" someone else. Each time a Rescuer sees a Victim as powerless, the Rescuer is not being truly loving or kind. Many Rescuers, fueled by insecurities, are trying to look good or do good to feel that their own lives have meaning. Some Rescuers become "martyrs," using quiet sighs or well-placed complaints to proclaim their heroic, unappreciated efforts. Eventually, though, a Rescuer becomes so tired of "fixing" the Victim's problems that s/he begins seeing the Victim as a Persecutor instead.

David Emerald explains, "One of the biggest temptations of people who want to help others, to make a contribution in the world, is to fall into the Victim Orientation role of Rescuer. It's one thing to lend a helping hand when someone has fallen but it's quite another to assume you have to walk on his or her behalf. A Rescuer sees the other person as a needy and powerless Victim. Rescuers breed dependence; they thrive on the need to be needed by a Victim."[127]

Those who know a person who is struggling can easily slip into the Rescuer role, validating the Victim's beliefs. It could happen when a brother tells his younger brother, "Your wife drinks all the time! There's no way you can cope with that! I'll take you fishing for a few weeks and get you out of this mess." Or, a single mom's friend says, "You poor thing; remembering your childhood abuse is more than anyone can handle. I'll move in with you. I'll take care of your kids and just let you cry as much as you need to." Neither person is helped by being treated like a helpless Victim.

When an individual assumes the emotional role of **Victim**, both **Rescuers and Persecutors** emerge, in various ways. A Persecutor could be another person, such as an abuser. A Persecutor often begins the cycle in the form of a real problem, such as a disease, long-term illness, a car crash, a failed marriage, a rebellious child, a natural disaster—or people who try to control your life, leaving you feeling like you've been hit by hurricane-force winds. But there is a significant difference between individuals who see themselves as "Victims" and those who are in a situation where they are "Victimized." Those who assume the Victim role believe their feelings of self-pity, helplessness, depression, and hurt are directly caused by their Persecutor(s), in whatever form a Persecutor appears in their lives. They surrender their right to choose their own response.

In the Victim Game, all three roles continue to shift, at different rates. One role might last for a week—or a year, but it can't last indefinitely. The Victim eventually has to see a Rescuer as a Persecutor. After all, if a successful rescue occurs, the Victim cannot stay in the familiar emotional status of Victim. Therefore, a Persecutor—in the form of a person, event, problem or circumstance—must emerge to keep the Victim "helpless," needing a new Rescuer.

80 CB

In the Victim Game, all three roles continue to shift, at different rates. One role might last for a week—or a year, but it can't last indefinitely. The Victim eventually has to see a Rescuer as a Persecutor.

80 CB

Transforming a Rescuer into a Persecutor isn't at all difficult for the practiced Victim. A few words, a few lies (which the Victim can convincingly make sound like truth), and the person who has been exhausted by prolonged futile attempts to bring deliverance to the Victim is suddenly viewed by others as the unkind, unfair, cruel or heartless individual the Victim crafts him or her to be.

Every role in this game is debilitating to every player! To stay out of harm's way, stay out of the game! If you realize you have been "playing" the role of Victim, Rescuer, or Persecutor, begin now to look for healthy roles in your relationships with others.

Based on your current understanding of the Victim Game, please read the following affirmation, and then rewrite it in your own words: *"The circumstances of life, the events of life, and the people around me in life do not make me the way I am, but reveal the way I am"* (Dr. Sam L. Peeples, Jr.).[128]

I think Dr. Peeples' statement means: _____

_____

_____

2. Day Two: **The Power of Choice**

To get out of the Victim Game, you can make new choices and learn new perspectives about your life. Instead of seeing yourself as Victim, learn to view yourself as a Creator. This distinction has been offered by David Emerald, author of *The Power of TED* (*The Empowerment Dynamic).

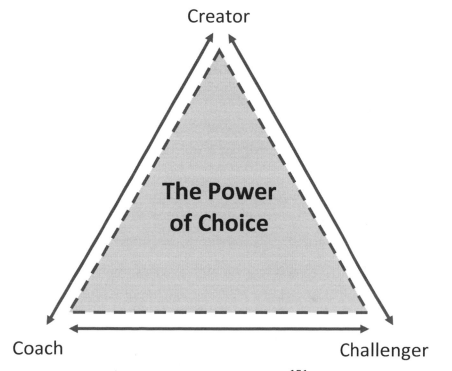

To get out of the Victim Game, you can make new choices and learn new perspectives about your life. Instead of seeing yourself as Victim, learn to view yourself as a Creator.

One significant difference between a Victim and a Creator is that a Creator realizes s/he has *choices* and can *make* choices about how to live life. A Victim and Creator can be facing similar problems, fears, concerns or difficulties, but the Creator chooses to look at problems as Challengers rather than as a person or event who is persecuting—or "out to get"—him or her. This is a profound difference! In addition, rather than looking for someone (or something) to rescue him or her, a Creator finds a Coach—perhaps in the form of a person, book, course, group or activity—to help the Creator discover and apply new perspectives to learn how to cope with a situation, problem or issue.

In other words, a Creator believes s/he has both the responsibility and opportunity to decide what to do about challenging situations, difficult people and genuine problems. When a Creator doesn't know how to tackle a problem or when s/he wants to learn new ways to grow, s/he finds a "Coach" to come alongside, with the unspoken assumption that the Creator is a human being capable of making wise choices, no matter how difficult the situation or concern.

The role of a Coach is quite unlike the Rescuer role. Instead of doing for an individual what s/he can do—or learn to do—a Coach helps the Creator grow and cope with a situation, problem or concern. The growth process might involve several coaches, each demonstrating respect for the Creator by giving input but not taking over his or her life.

A Coach helps a Creator see that living with Challengers is a positive part of life and growth, *whenever* Challengers appear in *whatever* form, whether people, circumstances, events or other concerns. A Creator learns to view Challengers as catalysts to change and growth rather than Persecutors delivering incapacitating defeat and misery. An internet search, a trip to the library, involvement in a Bible study or a call to a friend could help you as a Creator find positive coaching help.

If you identify yourself in the role of Victim and don't feel you have even one friend, this is a wonderful time to decide to become a person who can make and keep friends. With proper coaching and encouragement, you can move from Victim to Creator. There are growth groups available through community organizations, churches, and many other areas within society. They are as close to discovery as your daily newspaper or an internet search. If no people are available, there are thousands of books to help you expand your world. Reading the Bible can help you have wisdom to choose other positive books to read.

In the first book of the Bible, God established the Creator role, stating *"God created man in his own image, in the image of God he created him; male and female he created them. God blessed them and said to them, 'Be fruitful and increase in number; fill the earth and subdue it. Rule over the fish of the sea and the birds of the*

When a Creator doesn't know how to tackle a problem or when s/he wants to learn new ways to grow, s/he finds a "Coach" to come alongside, with the unspoken assumption that the Creator is a human being capable of making wise choices, no matter how difficult the situation or concern.

air and over every living creature that moves on the ground" (Genesis 1:27-28, NIV). Sometimes referred to as the Dominion Mandate, that passage describes each human being as remarkably created in God's image to subdue, rule or manage a specific domain. A Victim gives up, gives in or lets others walk over or decide for him or her. A Creator believes there is purpose for his or her unique existence. Review Psalm 139 to be reminded of your incredible design and worth.

There are surprising choices available to each of us when we view difficulties as challenging rather than as persecuting, debilitating or defeating. Accepting challenge as a part of life results in opening one's mind to discovering new ways to face the challenge instead of giving up or feeling there is no way to cope.

English poet John Milton said, "The mind is its own place, and in itself can make a Heaven of Hell, a Hell of Heaven." Describe how Milton's statement applies to the concepts of Victim and Creator. _____

_____

_____

_____

_____

_____

3. Day Three: **New Life Choices**

    Describe the main differences between the roles in the Victim Game (Karpman Triangle) and the Choice triangle. _____

    _____

    _____

    _____

    _____

    _____

    _____

    _____

    _____

    _____

    _____

    _____

    _____

    _____

After reviewing the roles in the Victim Game, please complete the following exercise. On the following page, **underline** the role(s) that currently apply to you. **Circle** the name of the role(s) you want to apply to your life.

80 CB

> Accepting challenge as a part of life results in opening one's mind to discovering new ways to face the challenge instead of giving up or feeling there is no way to cope.

80 CB

Compare and contrast the roles of **Victim** and **Creator**. _____

_____

_____

_____

_____

_____

_____

Compare and contrast the roles of **Rescuer** and **Coach**. _____

_____

_____

_____

_____

Standing in the position of Creator carries with it a great deal of responsibility, including how you respond to others. Most of humanity is still sleepwalking through life in the Victim Orientation.[129]

David Emerald

Compare and contrast the roles of **Persecutor** and **Challenger**. _____

_____

_____

_____

_____

_____

4.   Day Four: **Living in Peace**

Jesus spoke these words to his disciples: *These things I have spoken to you, so that in Me you may have peace. In the world you have tribulation, but take courage; I have overcome the world* (John 16:33, NASU).

As you think about Jesus' words, what choices will you make today to live as a Victor rather than a Victim?

_____

_____

_____

_____

_____

_____

_____

_____

_____

_____

Describe a Coach who could help you live as a Creator: _____

_____

_____

_____

_____

_____

Note: If your friend or family member was victimized through sexual abuse, you can provide creative coaching help by reviewing the five core areas of Competence, Security, Identity, Purpose and Belonging. Look for growth ideas in each core concern. Be careful not to move into Rescuer role when you see your loved one's pain. Instead, moment-by-moment, choose to live as a Creator in regard to your own life and concerns, becoming a Coach for others who request you support them via that role.

5. Day Five: **Being Creative**

Survivors of sexual abuse can again say, "I am a VICTOR!" Synonyms for the word "victor" include "winner, conqueror, vanquisher, champion and defeater." You, in Christ, are more than a conqueror (review Romans 8:37).

Realizing that you can live as a Creator today and for the rest of your life, you can focus on hope and healing, on the future rather than your past. This book has provided avenues to help you experience spiritual, emotional social and mental health. Applying new thought patterns to replace those damaged by molestation, you can keep moving into new ways of thinking and living.

God has good plans for your life. Please don't let your thoughts about your future be limited by your past—or even by the world's warped perspective of what is good. Each culture emphasizes different characteristics related to beauty; each culture has differing socio-economic standards; each culture has its own flaws and customs. Wherever you are in the world, the sum total of your earthly existence is described in Scripture as a "vanishing mist" or "vapor." Despite the brevity of our earthly lives, New Testament writers James and Peter remind us to consider our existence as having a creative eternal purpose.

Why, you do not even know what will happen tomorrow. What is your life? You are a mist that appears for a little while and then vanishes. Instead, you ought to say, "If it is the Lord's will, we will live and do this or that." James 4:14-15, NIV.

What a God we have! And how fortunate we are to have him, this Father of our Master Jesus! Because Jesus was raised from the dead, we've been given a brand-new life and have everything to live for, including a future in heaven—and the future

ೞ ಜ

Survivors of sexual abuse can say this: "I am a VICTOR!" Synonyms for the word "victor" include "winner, conqueror, vanquisher, champion and defeater." You, in Christ, are more than a conqueror.

ೞ ಜ

starts now! God is keeping careful watch over us and the future. The Day is coming when you'll have it all—life healed and whole. I know how great this makes you feel, even though you have to put up with every kind of aggravation in the meantime. Pure gold put in the fire comes out of it proved pure; genuine faith put through this suffering comes out proved genuine. When Jesus wraps this all up, it's your faith, not your gold, that God will have on display as evidence of his victory. You never saw him, yet you love him. You still don't see him, yet you trust him—with laughter and singing. Because you kept on believing, you'll get what you're looking forward to: total salvation. 1 Peter 1:3-9, THE MESSAGE.

How might you be helped by asking God to show you His creative will for each day? _____

_____

_____

_____

 Explore - God promises hope for your future. *"For I know the plans that I have for you,"* declares the Lord, *"plans for welfare and not for calamity to give you a future and a hope. Then you will call upon Me and come and pray to Me, and I will listen to you. You will seek Me and find Me when you search for Me with all your heart."*

Jeremiah 29:11-13, NASU

Take time to journal your thoughts to God as a prayer of thanksgiving.

_____

_____

_____

_____

_____

_____

_____

_____

_____

_____

 Week Eleven - Weekend Bonus Work:

Later Adulthood, ages 60 to 75, is when people usually reflect back on prior life stages, analyzing what they accomplished and where they failed.[130] It is important to think about the ninth stage of development before it occurs, so that you are ready to greet it with joy and hope. Introspection coupled with reflection on Truth results in increased wisdom and a sense of personal wholeness. During Later Adulthood, healthy development includes realizing that death is part of the life cycle, while

Many of life's failures are people who did not realize how close they were to success when they gave up.[131]

Thomas Edison

unhealthy development could include fearing death or not accepting it as part of the life cycle.

Negative self-examination during this stage about one's own or others' successes and failures can result in disdain. This, coupled with a tendency to blame others for personal choices, impedes progress. On the other hand, those who choose to integrate past experiences with positive steps can experience change and growth during Later Adulthood.

When people are experiencing despair at this stage, it often looks and feels like distrust, shame, guilt, or inferiority. Later Adulthood's core pathology of disdain is often portrayed in movies and television shows that feature humor that mocks people, disrespecting values or others' well-being.

To help develop positive choices in television or movie viewing habits, consider this: are the people you are watching on TV or in movies portraying values consistent with God's Word? Are they people you would invite into your home to teach you and your family or friends how to live? Are their ideas benefiting humanity or destroying it?

In light of these questions about making good choices about what I watch, I will:

_____
_____
_____
_____

Building a sense of integrity and respect for others requires consistent choices throughout life. What choices will you make today to demonstrate respect for others? _____

_____
_____
_____
_____

As people age, many are content to be "ordinary," not questioning status quo, simply doing what others do, watching what they watch and going where they go. It is important to pause and consider what you are doing, why you are doing it, and how it matters. You wrote your personal vision statement in chapter nine. How are you applying it this week? _____

_____
_____
_____
_____

Continuing to grow and learn throughout your life can help you avoid what is known as "the magnetism of mediocrity." Dr. Joseph "Tip" McFadden described

80 03
_____

When Jesus takes your hand, He keeps you tight. When Jesus keeps you tight, He leads you though your whole life. When Jesus leads you through your life, He brings you safely home.[132]

Corrie Ten Boom
_____
80 03

the magnetism of mediocrity as what happens when people who don't want to excel try to bring others down to their level. He says people who get a job and show up for work every day are in the top 50% of all workers. McFadden says those who "decide to do more than what is expected—those who have a sense of vision and responsibility, and do what NEEDS to be done, over and above what you are hired to do...soar into the top 10% of all workers!"[133]

Dr. McFadden says our main problems come from those "who have not made nor intend on making such a commitment to excellence. These ...'levelers' will try to bring you down to their level. The top 10%ers make the majority of workers stick out! The pressure coming from the majority, i.e., the levelers, is what I label the 'magnetism of mediocrity!' Watch out for the levelers!" urges Dr. McFadden. He says, "There is a powerful magnetic-like pull towards the center, or mediocrity."[134]

Describe ways you've noticed or experienced the "magnetism of mediocrity."

_____

_____

_____

Whether you work at home or in a career outside the home, you can choose to stay away from the pull toward mediocrity, reaching for the best God offers.

Today, how will you apply Philippians 3:14 to your life? *I press on toward the goal to win the prize for which God has called me heavenward in Christ Jesus* (NIV).

_____

_____

_____

_____

Make a commitment to keep growing and learning throughout life. On your healing journey, be careful not to allow "levelers" of circumstances, people, or events to slow you down or derail your progress. To keep you aware of levelers that could distract you, describe several choices you will make to keep living as a Creator every day.

_____

_____

_____

_____

_____

_____

_____

_____

_____

ℰℭ

Make a commitment to keep growing and learning throughout life. On your healing journey, be careful not to allow "levelers" of circumstances, people, or events to slow you down or derail your progress.

ℰℭ

Continuing to Heal

Chapter Twelve

Throughout the previous eleven lessons, you've discovered how to heal in the core of your being. You have learned how to be competent and secure; how to forgive; and how to know who you are. You have identified your purpose and discovered where you belong.

As you complete this season of healing, chapter 12 offers ideas to continue your progress for the rest of your life. Embracing new attitudes or moving away from old habits might be part of your ongoing growth. You will need to notice your thoughts and choices every single day for the rest of your life, because it is much easier to move backward than forward.

I understand *moving*, having lived in twenty-six different places since birth. Sometimes I've had difficulty making the mental and emotional transitions necessary to adapt to moves, navigating from coast to coast. However, in choosing to make positive transitions, I've discovered the joy of always discovering something new to learn! You, too, can continue learning and moving forward in your Core Healing journey. Don't be discouraged if the process seems challenging at times; determine to keep moving forward!

Sometimes my husband and I return to states where we once lived and drive slowly past former homes, remembering the joy our family shared there. But we are usually disappointed. Places where my husband created botanical masterpieces now only hint at the beauty they once displayed.

The biggest letdown was our California yard. Once owned by a landscape architect, it was a showplace of fruit-bearing trees, grape arbors, and terraces resplendent with everything from gigantic strawberries to the gentle scent of jasmine. When we returned, the yard was a barren wilderness. A huge evergreen had been savagely pruned so that it didn't even hint at its previous beauty. That yard could have been brought back to its original design, but it would have taken prolonged effort. All that would have been required, though, to keep the yard the way we left it was consistent maintenance.

When we moved from Colorado to Nebraska, we bought a 100-year-old house that had been neglected for years. A cracked fountain and unkempt yard barely hinted at its turn-of-the century beauty. Neighbors urged us to get professionals to help shape up the huge yard. Following their advice, we hired expert tree trimmers to prune overgrown ancient trees.

When the tree trimming crew arrived, the man known as Boss explained why extensive pruning was essential. Pointing emphatically to a large maple tree, he exuberantly explained, "There are two reasons these trees need to be pruned.

---

80 CR

Information without application leaves you in the same location. Make it your goal to greet each day with anticipation that you *can* apply new information and consistently move forward. Relocate your mind and emotions to keep experiencing growth.

80 CR

One: insect infestation! If you don't trim the excess foliage, your trees are going to be destroyed by insects that get inside them! The other reason: storms. If the wind can't blow through a tree, a storm will knock it down!"

Inside the house, listening to chain saws ripping through huge branches, I thought about a parallel in the Christian life. If God doesn't "prune" my life, I can be destroyed either by something in me—an attitude, a thought pattern or a behavior—or by something outside of me, like the "storms" of life.

Suddenly, I remembered that I didn't ask the tree crew not to prune my favorite tree, a linden sprawling near our back door. No one knew, but I looked at that tree whenever I missed the majestic mountains of Colorado and my friends there. Every time I noticed one exquisite branch swaying in the breeze, sunlight shimmering on its leaves, I thought of it as my "comfort branch."

I ran outside just in time to see Boss finishing off the comfort branch with his chain saw. As the beautiful branch toppled to the ground with a decisive thud, I burst into tears. The gruff foreman climbed down, clearly puzzled. "What's wrong, lady?" he asked. I stammered something about how much I liked that branch, trying not to look where it lay, destroyed. The foreman spoke decisively, "Lady, that branch had to go; it was dead!"

For comfort, I had been turning to something dead. Walking into the house and drying my tears, I asked God to forgive me for trying to find comfort in something that clearly could not provide it. I turned to Him, remembering the lesson of pruning in John 15.

Later that afternoon, my neighbor knocked on my back door—the one looking out on the now-bereft tree. She enthused, "I had to come tell you how beautiful your house looks from across the street at my house! You know where that big branch was?" I nodded. Pointing at the gaping space, she continued, "With that out of the way, sunlight is streaming across your house! It's like God's light is covering your house!"

When a pruner got rid of my silly source of comfort, light replaced something dead with joy others could share. As my life continued to move forward, I learned new ways to put my hope in God and reach out to other people with His love.

There might be "dead things" in your life still. You can ask God, the master gardener, to lovingly remove them so you are free to enjoy His peace, comfort, hope and strength. This chapter will provide practical steps to help you continually recognize God's fresh new lessons for your life.

"Continuing to Heal" reviews basic five areas of Core Healing as introduced in chapter one: Competence, Security, Identity, Purpose and Belonging, focusing on healing goals associated with all five core concerns.

I am the true vine, and My Father is the vinedresser. Every branch in Me that does not bear fruit He takes away; and every branch that bears fruit He prunes, that it may bear more fruit.

John 15:1-2, NKJV

1. Day One: **Competence,** considered in chapter four, "Are We Having FUD Yet?"

    Core Healing Goal: to establish new beliefs which result in self-respect and competence.

    Chapter four explained how to replace inaccurate core beliefs about being less than others. You learned to replace negative self-talk with positive self-talk, applying God's opinion of you instead of false beliefs. You realized that your life no longer needs to be dominated by the painful FUD trifecta of Fear, Uncertainty and Doubt.

    To keep practicing positive self-talk, it is helpful to continue regular journaling, working on positive replacement thoughts instead of rehashing debilitating negative self-talk. A superb way to journal is to write down your response to specific Scripture verses or passages. If you live where someone might read (and disrespect) your private thoughts, you can shred the pages after you write them.

    As you journal to various Scripture passages, you can use the following questions as a guide:

    ✓ What do I see?

    ✓ What does it mean?

    ✓ How can I apply it to my life?

    ✓ Are there promises for me to claim?

    ✓ Are there sins I need to confess?

    Appendix D provides a journaling page listing the above questions, as well as ideas to help you study and apply God's Word.

    Following is a sample journaling exercise, applying John 15:1-5 to my "comfort branch" experience described on pages 159-160.

    ¹I am the true vine, and My Father is the vinedresser. ²Every branch in Me that does not bear fruit, He takes away; and every branch that bears fruit, He prunes it so that it may bear more fruit. ³You are already clean because of the word which I have spoken to you. ⁴"Abide in Me, and I in you. As the branch cannot bear fruit of itself unless it abides in the vine, so neither can you unless you abide in Me. ⁵I am the vine, you are the branches; he who abides in Me and I in him, he bears much fruit, for apart from Me you can do nothing. John 15:1-5, NASU

In response to John 15:1-5, I wrote the following.

What do I see?

Jesus is speaking; He calls Himself the true Vine. That means He is my life source. He refers to His Father as the "Vinedresser," the one who prunes branches to make them bear more fruit. He also says His Word makes us clean. As I abide in Him, I will bear fruit—much fruit. Galatians 5:22-23 lists some of the fruit He promises to bear in and through my life: love, joy, peace, patience, kindness, goodness, faithfulness, gentleness and self-control

What does it mean?

It means I am to quit relying on my limited human strength; God has done everything that needs to be done to make me free to live a life that has meaning, in Him. It means I can rely on His infinite strength; He will provide every resource needed for what He leads me to do.

How can I apply it to my life?

I can quit looking at meaningless things like branches to give me comfort, relying on God instead. I can be hopeful each day, knowing God has a good plan to make my life bear fruit for His glory. When I suffer painful losses, I can be confident that God's pruning is for my good. I can apply John 15 by realizing God is the Vine—the unfailing source of strength, joy, grace and hope; I am a branch and can simply "hang out" in Him. I will keep spending time in the Word every day, growing in Him, learning to live what He says.

Are there promises to claim?

Verse 4, "Abide in Me, and I in you" reminds me that Jesus lives inside me, giving me everything I need for each day. He promises that my life will bear fruit, so I can trust Him to produce in me the fruit described in Galatians 5:22-23, allowing God to exhibit His perfect workmanship (per Ephesians 2:10) through my life.

Are there sins to confess?

God, I confess that I settled for empty things of this world instead of fully relying on You. Help me keep my heart fully focused on You, confident that You promise to provide for all my needs—including relational, emotional, physical, intellectual and spiritual concerns. Lord, direct each step I take so that I'll do what You want me to do. (At the time the event happened, I confessed to both my husband and our neighbor the foolish way I briefly looked to a finite tree for comfort instead of to our infinite God.)

Martyn Lloyd-Jones explains the process of confessing sin. "If we find the sin, if we have found the fault, if we have found slackness or anything that is wrong or unworthy we must go at once and confess it honestly and completely to God. That is a vital part of the exercises, and we shall never get well until we carry it out. God commands us to do this, so let us do it. Let us go straight to Him. It may also involve going to somebody else, it may mean apologizing, it may mean confessing something. It does not always mean this, but if God tells us to do it we must do it."[137]

Make copies of the biblical journaling form in Appendix D, or use a notebook of your own to begin your journaling process. As you journal, respond to each question listed on the form and on page 161.

 Explore - Use the following passages to begin journaling your journey of hope related to **Competence**.

Nehemiah 8:10	Matthew 5:1-16
Isaiah 26:3	Romans 15:13-14
Lamentations 3:21-26	2 Corinthians 3:5
Micah 6:8	2 Timothy 2:1-2

You can search Scripture and find hundreds of additional passages, and you can ask others who are familiar with the Bible to help your search. You can ask God to guide you. In James 1:5, God promises to provide wisdom to those who ask Him in faith. *But if any of you lacks wisdom, let him ask of God, who gives to all generously and without reproach, and it will be given to him. But he must ask in faith without any doubting, for the one who doubts is like the surf of the sea, driven and tossed by the wind.* James 1:5-6, NASU

Be a Creator by being proactive to continue building competence. Many areas offer classes that can help you gain expertise in numerous subjects. For example, if you've always wanted to write a book, you could sign up for a creative writing class at a local college or online university. If you want to increase your computer skills, you could take a computer class. If you have trouble talking with people, there are classes and groups that offer assistance in expanding communication skills. You could even check out YouTube for help cultivating various interests—it contains lessons on everything from gardening to knitting to playing the xylophone [there are also lessons you wouldn't want to learn, so use discretion]. If your area offers Bible studies, you might find a study group to help you grow.

2. Day Two: **Security**

Core Healing Goal: to move from attitudes or actions shaped by abuse into the safety and security God provides by making healing choices each day.

Chapter Five, "Name Your Tyrant," helped you learn how to experience security. New ways of thinking helped you move completely away from the emotional power and control your abuser exerted over you, into the safety of God's love.

Continue journaling as outlined on day one. As you do, ask God to affirm your sense of security in Him.

 Explore - Use the following passages to begin journaling your journey of hope, safety and **Security**.

Psalm 4:7-8   Isaiah 43:1-7

Psalm 34   Philippians 4:13

Proverbs 18:10   1 John 5:11-15

You can increase your sense of safety by living in the present moment. Though it is vital to pray, prepare and plan, worrying about tomorrow robs today of its strength.

A simple exercise to help you enjoy the moment is to take a mini-vacation. This vacation costs nothing and requires no packing or preparation. All you need to do is make time for a 15-minute nature walk. You can do this at a park, in your neighborhood, at a beach, or anywhere else in nature where you feel safe. Simply set aside a few moments from your normal activities to gain perspective. Throughout your 15-minute walk, observe everything you can, using all five senses. Let yourself enjoy the moment, breathing deeply and fully noticing your surroundings. When you return from your walk, **write down everything you saw, heard, smelled, touched or tasted** in the space below. (Do not write during your walk; it is time to observe and enjoy.) _____

_____

_____

_____

_____

_____

_____

_____

_____

_____

_____

_____

_____

Were you surprised by how much you noticed during your walk that you might ordinarily not have observed at all? _____ Yes _____ No Describe your thoughts and emotions. _____

_____

_____

_____

_____

Living in God's security is a reality; noticing what He has given you requires persistent awareness and conscious effort, just as it did to notice life with your five senses. Make one ambition to simply notice God's goodness each day.

Appendix E (p. 181) offers Grounding Exercises to help you experience safety and security.

3. Day Three: **Identity**, described in chapter eight, *Who Am I?*

Core Healing Goal: to recognize five areas of identity and learn how to grow in each area.

Chapter eight emphasized that finding fulfillment in God helps you know who you are created to be. It is important not to allow individuality—too much focus on "self"—to blur your uniquely-designed personality. Oswald Chambers describes personality as "infinitely more" than individuality, stating "Individuality is the characteristic of the natural man, personality is the characteristic of the spiritual man."[138] D. Martyn Lloyd-Jones, wrote "We are given different temperaments by God. Yes, but it must never be true of us as Christians that we are controlled by our temperaments. We must be controlled by the Holy Ghost."[139]

Your personality can blossom in response to the Person of God as you respond to His love instead of your fears. You can live by faith in His goodness rather than in despair of the past.

To continue developing in the ways God designed, it is important to realize the difference between a *natural* person and a *spiritual* person.

The natural person is described in Galatians 5:17-21, AMP [17]*For the desires of the flesh are opposed to the [Holy] Spirit, and the [desires of the] Spirit are opposed to the flesh (godless human nature); for these are antagonistic to each other [continually withstanding and in conflict with each other], so that you are not free but are prevented from doing what you desire to do. [18]But if you are guided (led) by the [Holy] Spirit, you are not subject to the Law. [19]Now the doings (practices) of the flesh are clear (obvious): they are immorality, impurity, indecency, [20]idolatry, sorcery, enmity, strife, jealousy, anger (ill temper), selfishness, divisions (dissensions), party spirit*

荒荓

"Accepted in the beloved."

What a state of privilege! It includes our justification before God, but the term "acceptance" in the Greek means more than that. It signifies that we are the objects of divine complacence, nay, even of divine delight.[140]

Charles Spurgeon

荒荓

(factions, sects with peculiar opinions, heresies), ^{21}*envy, drunkenness, carousing, and the like. I warn you beforehand, just as I did previously, that those who do such things shall not inherit the kingdom of God.*

What do you notice in verses 17-21 about how people live when they are controlling themselves? _____

_____

_____

_____

_____

_____

_____

_____

In contrast, verses 22-25 outline how we live when we allow the Holy Spirit to take charge of our lives. ^{22}*But the fruit of the [Holy] Spirit [the work which His presence within accomplishes] is love, joy (gladness), peace, patience (an even temper, forbearance), kindness, goodness (benevolence), faithfulness,* ^{23} *gentleness (meekness, humility), self-control (self-restraint, continence). Against such things there is no law [that can bring a charge].* ^{24}*And those who belong to Christ Jesus (the Messiah) have crucified the flesh (the godless human nature) with its passions and appetites and desires.* ^{25}*If we live by the [Holy] Spirit, let us also walk by the Spirit. [If by the Holy Spirit we have our life in God, let us go forward walking in line, our conduct controlled by the Spirit.]* Galatians 5:22-25, AMP

Using Galatians 5 as a litmus test of identity, write about what you want your life to exhibit.

_____

_____

_____

_____

_____

_____

_____

_____

_____

_____

_____

_____

ഽ ൘

If our selfish hearts are trying to trick us into feeling a false sense of dissatisfaction, a good strong dose of thanksgiving will cure what ails us.[141]

Beth Moore

ഽ ൘

Continue journaling as outlined on day one. As you do, ask God to affirm your sense of identity in Him.

 Explore - Use the following passages for journaling your journey of hope related to **Identity**. As you consider each passage, ask yourself "How does God see me?"

Psalm 139:13-15   2 Corinthians 5:17-18

Zephaniah 3:17   Ephesians 2:1-10

John 1:12   Colossians 3:1-12

Romans 8:17-18   1 Thessalonians 1:4-6

4. Day Four: **Purpose**

Core Healing Goal: to understand and articulate your life purpose.

Knowing your life has meaning, you can mentally and emotionally let go of past suffering, choosing to move forward instead. You can enjoy what God provides each day of your life. When you face new challenges, you can keep moving forward with confidence that you can grow amidst pain, continually becoming stronger than you were before. It is vital to keep building on solid foundational beliefs that supply consistent purpose for your life.

Martyn Lloyd-Jones was minister of Westminster Chapel in London for twenty-five years and wrote more than thirty books. In the book *Why Does God Allow Suffering?* he wrote, "According to the New Testament there is but one real happiness or joy, and that is the happiness that is based upon a true relationship to God, the happiness which is the result of the righteousness that God gives us through Jesus Christ His Son. It is because we have false notions of happiness, and base it upon false and insecure foundations, that we so constantly experience alternating periods of elation and dejection, joy and despair. The only joy that never fails is that which is given by the Lord Himself according to His promise. The way to obtain it, and to retain it, therefore, is to understand and to grasp the conditions on which He gives it."[142]

Review chapter nine. Are there any changes you want to make to your personal vision statement on page 127? _____ Yes _____ No Rewrite your vision/statement of purpose here, adding changes if desired. _____

_____

_____

_____

_____

_____

_____

_____

ᏚᎧ ᏟᎶ

When God created you, He built into you all the natural necessities for performing and fulfilling your purposed assignment. Everyone possesses natural inherent traits that are required for their purpose. In essence, you are the ***way*** you are because of the ***why*** you are.[143]

Myles Munroe

ᏚᎧ ᏟᎶ

Continue journaling as outlined on day one. As you do, ask God to affirm your sense of purpose in Him.

Explore - Use the following passages for journaling your journey of hope related to **Purpose**. As you consider each passage, ask yourself "How has God designed me and what is His purpose for my life?"

1 Chronicles 16:26-29	Ephesians 1:11-14
Psalm 68:1-6	Ephesians 2:10
Psalm 73:23-28	Philippians 2:1-4
Galatians 1:3-5	2 Peter 3:18

5. Day Five: **Belonging**

Core Healing Goal: to understand and identify where you belong.

Chapter Ten repeatedly emphasizes that we already belong—forever—in Jesus. He understands rejection—people rejected Him so totally that they crucified Him. You can trust Jesus' promises to provide for your needs.

Charles Haddon Spurgeon described the prayer of the psalmist in Psalm 12:1, and its plea, "Help, Lord." Spurgeon said "the prayer itself is remarkable...David mourned the fewness of faithful men, and therefore lifted his heart in supplication—when the creature failed, he flew to the Creator. He evidently felt his own weakness, or he would not have cried for help." Spurgeon continued, "*The answer to the prayer is certain,* if it be sincerely offered through Jesus. The Lord's character assures us that He will not leave His people; His relationship as Father and Husband guarantee us His aid; His gift of Jesus is a pledge of every good thing; and His sure promise stands, "Fear not, I WILL HELP THEE....In Him our help is found."[144]

We always belong in Him; we can always cry out to Him. God knows our need for companionship, for understanding, for community; He created us for community. When friends fail, He will not fail. *The Lord's lovingkindnesses indeed never cease, for His compassions never fail. They are new every morning; great is Your faithfulness.* (Lamentations 3:22-23, NASU)

When we don't feel like we belong, we can easily be tempted to give up. In his book *Shattered Dreams*, author Larry Crabb described how "the Holy Spirit uses the pain of our shattered dreams to help us discover our desire for God, to help us begin dreaming the highest dream."[145]

"In our deceived culture, we must grasp the truth of what God is now doing in our lives or we will miss the joy of Christianity," said Crabb. "God is *not*

Let the morning bring me word of your unfailing love, for I have put my trust in you. Show me the way I should go, for to you I lift up my soul.

Psalm 143:8, NIV

168

cooperating with us to make life work so we can feel now all that He has created us to feel. But many people think He is. They think that's His job. There are two problems with that view. *One*, better circumstances, whether winning the lottery or saving your marriage, can never produce the joy we were designed to experience. Only an intimate relationship with Perfect Love can provide that joy. *Two*, in this life, we can never feel what God intended us to feel, at least not in full measure. To be completely happy, we must experience perfect intimacy with Perfect Love *and* every second-thing blessing that Perfect Love can provide. In this life, we have neither. God will provide both, but not till heaven."[146]

God designed each of us to belong, to be part of a community of caring believers. But it is important not to base your sense of worth on others, who can easily choose not to treat you the way God designed for you to be treated. No matter what happens, we can continue learning and growing, developing healthy ways to relate with others. When others hurt us, we can turn to God for healing and new hope, realizing we are not alone in the struggle to belong.

Clients often ask me if I were sexually abused. I remember a time when I was about four years old, when a fifty-something relative asked me to come into his bedroom to see his pet monkey.

I remember following him into his room and into his walk-in closet. I remember feeling betrayed, becoming acutely aware that he lied to me. There was no pet monkey. I also remember being afraid of that relative afterwards and never wanting to go back to that room.

Years ago, trying to remember details related to that incident, I asked God to show me what really happened. He led me to pray Psalm 139:23-24.

Search me, O God, and know my heart; try me and know my anxious thoughts; and see if there be any hurtful way in me, and lead me in the everlasting way (NASU).

God didn't reveal further details to me, so I quit wondering what might have happened. Many years later, while facilitating a counseling group for abuse survivors, I learned that some people use the slang term "monkey" to describe male genitals.

Trusting God to heal unknown areas of life, I asked Him to use that situation and my feelings about it for His glory. Perhaps this book is an answer to that prayer, helping us learn how to experience His faithful leading of each of us "in the everlasting way."

If you have experienced trauma and can't remember details of what happened, perhaps Psalm 139:23-24 would be an encouraging prayer for you, too. You can safely entrust your hurts to God. One of His Hebrew names is YAHWEH ROPHE, The LORD Who Heals (see Exodus 15:26).

    ℘ ℘

> God designed each of us to belong, to be part of a community of caring believers. But it is important not to base your sense of worth on others, who can easily choose not to treat you the way God designed for you to be treated.

    ℘ ℘

Continue journaling as outlined on day one. As you do, ask God to affirm your sense of belonging in Him.

 Explore - Use the following passages to record your journey of hope related to **Belonging**. As you consider each passage, remind yourself "I do belong forever, through the Lord Jesus Christ."

1 Samuel 16:7

Psalm 25

Psalm 103

Psalm 142

Romans 1:6

1 Corinthians 12:12-27

Philippians 4:2-8

2 Timothy 1:7

 Weekend Bonus Work:

Very Old Age, the tenth stage of psychosocial development, occurs from age 75 until death.[147]   Individuals cope with changes in their aging bodies as they near the end of their earthly existence. When sexual abuse occurs during this stage of development, many people give up. Even during Very Old Age, confidence can be regained through intentional focus on God instead of abuse. Otherwise, total introversion or withdrawal can occur in an individual who is molested in Very Old Age or in someone who has not yet healed from prior abuse.

In general, even without sexual abuse, many people fear the aging process, knowing their bodies will no longer do what they once did. For Christians, this stage of life is not to be dreaded but anticipated, because we know we're closer to being in the presence of our loving Lord. Our finite existence will be transformed into an infinite existence, where all suffering, pain and sorrow will disappear.

1 Corinthians 15:53-57 (NIV) describes the process of moving from earthly to heavenly existence. *For the perishable must clothe itself with the imperishable, and the mortal with immortality. When the perishable has been clothed with the imperishable, and the mortal with immortality, then the saying that is written will come true: "Death has been swallowed up in victory." "Where, O death, is your victory? Where, O death, is your sting?" The sting of death is sin, and the power of sin is the law. But thanks be to God! He gives us the victory through our Lord Jesus Christ.*

The victory Paul describes in 1 Corinthians is a victory you can experience at every stage of life. You don't have to wait until you die to live in the victory Christ won for you! Because sin delivers the "sting of death," it is important for you to know—wherever you are now—that you have been delivered from sin.

> For Christians, this stage of life is not to be dreaded but anticipated, because we know we're closer to being in the presence of our loving Lord.

A Letter from the Author

Dear Reader,

I am praying for you, with thankfulness that we could meet with one another in these pages. I pray that you will experience God's tender healing throughout the rest of your life. God promises this: *For sin shall not have dominion over you, for you are not under law but under grace.* (Romans 6:14, NKJV). Dominion indicates power and control.

There was a time when your abuser exercised power over you—that power is DONE, FINISHED, ENDED! Your molester's sinful behavior no longer controls your emotions, intellect, body, spirit or relationships. You are free to live as a whole person, in God's grace, strength, mercy and peace! Your core healing has taken you away from the damage of the past into the promises God has for the rest of your life.

Centuries ago, God spoke to Cyrus, promising to "go before you and make the crooked places straight; I will break in pieces the gates of bronze and cut the bars of iron. I will give you the treasures of darkness and hidden riches of secret places, that you may know that I, the LORD, who call you by your name, Am the God of Israel" (Isaiah 45:2-3, NKJV).

When God called Cyrus, it was surprisingly personal. An idol-worshipping pagan, Cyrus was called by God to accomplish a specific purpose regarding God's chosen people, Israel. Matthew Henry writes that "Some tell us that in his infancy he was an outcast, left exposed, and was saved from perishing by a herdsman's wife." God can use outcasts—people the world doesn't even notice—to accomplish His purpose.

God's call to you is personal, too. He calls you by name; He wants to break down barriers to your core healing. He offers the riches of His Presence so you can live in confident assurance of His love every day. In these pages, I hope you've experienced His unfailing love for you.

I'm glad we could travel together in your journey of hope. Now, I pray you'll continue walking forward in the safety and hope God offers just for you.

May the God of your hope so fill you with all joy and peace in believing [through the experience of your faith] that by the power of the Holy Spirit you may abound and be overflowing (bubbling over) with hope. Romans 15:13, AMP

In His Matchless Love,

Marti

Replacing Distorted Thoughts with Biblical Perspectives

As you consider the various types of distorted thinking delineated in chapter three, reflect on your own thought processes. When you realize you are experiencing emotions such as anxiety, depression, anger, fear or worry, STOP and take time to reflect on what you were thinking about before those feelings occurred. When you identify a cognitive distortion, repeatedly think about the Scripture verses listed following each type of distortion instead of reverting to old attitude or beliefs. You can also search your Bible or a free online Scripture source (such as www.biblegateway.com) for hundreds of other verses about each of your areas of concern.

Memorizing and meditating on Scripture can help you develop new thought processes. As you consider the verses on the following pages, you can apply the Glance/Gaze Principle delineated in Matthew 6:25-34 (NIV).

"Therefore I tell you, do not worry about your life, what you will eat or drink; or about your body, what you will wear. Is not life more important than food, and the body more important than clothes? Look at the birds of the air; they do not sow or reap or store away in barns, and yet your heavenly Father feeds them. Are you not much more valuable than they? Who of you by worrying can add a single hour to his life?

And why do you worry about clothes? See how the lilies of the field grow. They do not labor or spin. Yet I tell you that not even Solomon in all his splendor was dressed like one of these. If that is how God clothes the grass of the field, which is here today and tomorrow is thrown into the fire, will he not much more clothe you, O you of little faith? So do not worry, saying, 'What shall we eat?' or 'What shall we drink?' or 'What shall we wear?' For the pagans run after all these things, and your heavenly Father knows that you need them. But seek first his kingdom and his righteousness, and all these things will be given to you as well. Therefore do not worry about tomorrow, for tomorrow will worry about itself. Each day has enough trouble of its own."

Picture Jesus, walking with His disciples. Smiling, He points out birds flying overhead as He talks about God's provision for every need. He doesn't tell His children to ignore needs or problems. He doesn't encourage us to deny that challenges exist. Instead, He teaches a better way in Matthew 6:33–the Glance/Gaze Principle. This principle explains how to Glance at our needs and problems (so we don't live in a state of denial) and then Gaze at Jesus, entrusting all of our needs, challenges and difficulties to His perfect care.

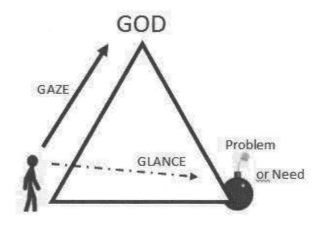

As you choose what you think about, you are essentially choosing to glance at your concerns rather than be dominated by them. The verses on the following pages give practical ideas of how to gaze at God in the midst of challenges, problems, needs or distress. And, there are hundreds of other verses not listed here that you can discover in God's Word to help with your specific areas of concern!

Changing your thought processes requires conscious, deliberate choices to meditate on the truth that can set you free from debilitating patterns of thinking, feeling and living. You can open your Bible and allow God to give you healing thought processes instead of repeating old lies over and over. For example, if you woke up today and looked in the mirror, focusing on a perceived flaw, you can look in Psalm 139 and repeat the truth stated in verse 14: "God says I am fearfully and wonderfully made!" Believing that truth can help you overcome lies that keep you trapped in discouragement and despair.

Chapter three describes ten types of distorted thinking, each of which is reviewed on the following pages. As you make conscious choices about what you think, you will likely notice corresponding changes in your feelings and behavior. [There are some exceptions: illness, medications, brain injury and other factors can affect your thoughts and emotions, too.]

Emotional Reasoning - Though emotions can be legitimate indicators of real concerns, when thoughts are distorted by emotional reasoning, the result can be depression, anxiety and even despair. When you are aware of this type of distorted thinking, **you can choose** not to believe everything your emotions tell you. As you begin to journal and want to find "New Healing Thoughts," the following Scripture passages can give you thoughts on which to focus to help you experience joy, peace and hope.

The Lord is my shepherd; I shall not want. He makes me to lie down in green pastures; He leads me beside the still waters. He restores my soul; He leads me in the paths of righteousness for His name's sake. Yea, though I walk through the valley of the shadow of death, I will fear no evil; For You are with me; Your rod and Your staff, they comfort me. You prepare a table before me in the presence of my enemies; You anoint my head with oil; My cup runs over. Surely goodness and mercy shall follow me all the days of my life; And I will dwell in the house of the Lord forever. Psalm 23, NKJV

For we walk by faith [we regulate our lives and conduct ourselves by our conviction or belief respecting man's relationship to God and divine things, with trust and holy fervor; thus we walk] not by sight or appearance. 2 Corinthians 5:7, AMP

When doubts filled my mind, your comfort gave me renewed hope and cheer. Psalm 94:19, NLT

Why are you down in the dumps, dear soul? Why are you crying the blues? Fix my eyes on God—soon I'll be praising again. He puts a smile on my face. He's my God. When my soul is in the dumps, I rehearse everything I know of you, From Jordan depths to Hermon heights, including Mount Mizar. Psalm 42:5-6, THE MESSAGE

Jumping to Conclusions - Instead of reacting to what you think or assume happened, was said or meant by another person, you can try to understand the other person's perspective. You can ask questions about what you think you heard, such as the open-ended, "Help me understand..." You can keep your body language calm so that the other person feels safe talking with you. Instead of believing the worst about what someone thinks about you, you can realize you are loved by God. When you allow His love to overflow your heart, you are less likely to believe others are out to get you. And, even when others are against you, you can experience God's peace (see Isaiah 26:3).

Hear my words, you wise men; listen to me, you men of learning. For the ear tests words as the tongue tastes food. Let us discern for ourselves what is right; let us learn together what is good. Job 34:2-4, NIV

He who answers before listening—that is his folly and his shame. Proverbs 18:13, NIV

My dear brothers, take note of this: Everyone should be quick to listen, slow to speak and slow to become angry, for man's anger does not bring about the righteous life that God desires. James 1:19-20, ESV

My dear friends, don't believe everything you hear. Carefully weigh and examine what people tell you. Not everyone who talks about God comes from God. There are a lot of lying preachers loose in the world. 1 John 4:1, THE MESSAGE

All or Nothing Thinking - Someone once said that the difficulty of perfectionism isn't really that we're trying to be *like* God; it's that we're trying to *be* God. If you look at life through the lens of needing to be in control of circumstances or of people, you'll likely be disappointed a great deal of the time. Asking God to open your mind to fresh ideas can provide new perspective.

Open up before God, keep nothing back; he'll do whatever needs to be done: He'll validate your life in the clear light of day and stamp you with approval at high noon. Psalm 37:5-6, THE MESSAGE

A man's mind plans his way, but the Lord directs his steps and makes them sure. Proverbs 16:9, AMP

And He has said to me, "My grace is sufficient for you, for power is perfected in weakness." Most gladly, therefore, I will rather boast about my weaknesses, so that the power of Christ may dwell in me. Therefore I am well content with weaknesses, with insults, with distresses, with persecutions, with difficulties, for Christ's sake; for when I am weak, then I am strong. 2 Corinthians 12:9-10, NASU

Always be joyful. Never stop praying. Be thankful in all circumstances, for this is God's will for you who belong to Christ Jesus. 1 Thessalonians 5:16-18, NLT

Should Thinking - God is a God of hope, of renewal, conviction and LIFE—not of condemnation. As you allow Him to encourage your soul, you can release "should" thinking to His limitless love. Doing what you **can** do in His strength, you can stop mentally beating yourself up about what you "should" do.

And so each of us shall give an account of himself [give an answer in reference to judgment] to God. Then let us no more criticize and blame and pass judgment on one another, but rather decide and endeavor never to put a stumbling block or an obstacle or a hindrance in the way of a brother. So let us then definitely aim for and eagerly pursue what makes for harmony and for mutual upbuilding (edification and development) of one another. Romans 14:12-13;19, AMP

Not that I have already obtained all this, or have already been made perfect, but I press on to take hold of that for which Christ Jesus took hold of me. Brothers, I do not consider myself yet to have taken hold of it. But one thing I do: Forgetting what is behind and straining toward what is ahead, I press on toward the goal to win the prize for which God has called me heavenward in Christ Jesus.

All of us who are mature should take such a view of things. And if on some point you think differently, that too God will make clear to you. Only let us live up to what we have already attained. Philippians 3:12-16, NIV

I know how to live on almost nothing or with everything. I have learned the secret of living in every situation, whether it is with a full stomach or empty, with plenty or little. For I can do everything through Christ, who gives me strength. Philippians 4:12-14, NLT

Overgeneralization - Looking at life through the lens of God's Word can bring an entirely different focus to all of life. Instead of seeing "normal" as what you have known, you can allow God to give you His original definition for your life—one that isn't fueled by old generalized thought patterns.

Trust in the Lord and do good; dwell in the land and enjoy safe pasture. Delight yourself in the Lord and he will give you the desires of your heart. Commit your way to the Lord; trust in him and he will do this: He will make your righteousness shine like the dawn, the justice of your cause like the noonday sun. Psalm 37:3-6, NIV

O Lord, you have searched me and you know me. You know when I sit and when I rise; you perceive my thoughts from afar. You discern my going out and my lying down; you are familiar with all my ways. Before a word is on my tongue you know it completely, O Lord. Psalm 139:1-4, NIV

Be joyful always; pray continually; give thanks in all circumstances, for this is God's will for you in Christ Jesus. 1 Thessalonians 5:16-18, NIV

Catastrophizing - When your automatic thoughts focus on disaster, tragedy, or on past, present or future suffering, it is difficult to enjoy today. God's Word offers hope in the midst of all circumstances, conditions and situations. You can train your thoughts to rest in Him.

GOD IS our Refuge and Strength [mighty and impenetrable to temptation], a very present and well-proved help in trouble. Therefore we will not fear, though the earth should change and though the mountains be shaken into the midst of the seas, though its waters roar and foam, though the mountains tremble at its swelling and tumult. Selah [pause, and calmly think of that]! There is a river whose streams shall make glad the city of God, the holy place of the tabernacles of the Most High. God is in the midst of her, she shall not be moved; God will help her right early [at the dawn of the morning]. The nations raged, the kingdoms tottered and were moved; He uttered His voice, the earth melted. The Lord of hosts is with us; the God of Jacob is our Refuge (our Fortress and High Tower). Selah [pause, and calmly think of that]! Psalm 46:1-7, AMP

Cast your cares on the Lord and he will sustain you; he will never let the righteous fall. Psalm 55:22, NIV

When my anxious thoughts multiply within me, Your consolations delight my soul. Psalm 94:19, NASU

But now, God's Message, the God who made you in the first place, Jacob, the One who got you started, Israel: Don't be afraid, I've redeemed you. I've called your name. You're mine.

When you're in over your head, I'll be there with you. When you're in rough waters, you will not go down. When you're between a rock and a hard place, it won't be a dead end—Because I am God, your personal God, The Holy of Israel, your Savior. Isaiah 43:1-3a, THE MESSAGE

Filtering - This type of distorted thinking occurs when you minimize positive events, statements or people and maximize negative words, interactions or circumstances. If you have allowed your mind to park on negativity, you can make a conscious effort to renew your mind with God's Word. If you think this is too big of a challenge, keep in mind that you will succeed when you rely on God's limitless strength rather than your weaknesses.

Finally, brethren, whatever is true, whatever is honorable, whatever is right, whatever is pure, whatever is lovely, whatever is of good repute, if there is any excellence and if anything worthy of praise, dwell on these things. Philippians 4:8, NASU

IF THEN you have been raised with Christ [to a new life, thus sharing His resurrection from the dead], aim at and seek the [rich, eternal treasures] that are above, where Christ is, seated at the right hand of God. And set your minds and keep them set on what is above (the higher things), not on the things that are on the earth. For [as far as this world is concerned] you have died, and your [new, real] life is hidden with Christ in God. Colossians 3:1-3, AMP

Therefore, since we are surrounded by such a great cloud of witnesses, let us throw off everything that hinders and the sin that so easily entangles, and let us run with perseverance the race marked out for us. Let us fix our eyes on Jesus, the author and perfecter of our faith, who for the joy set before him endured the cross, scorning its shame, and sat down at the right hand of the throne of God. Hebrews 12:1-3, NIV

Blaming & Labeling - The best way to avoid living in a state of continual criticism and blame—either of yourself or others—is to focus on God rather than yourself, your problems, or others. Practice the "Glance → Gaze" approach of thinking.

For the Lord God is a Sun and Shield; the Lord bestows [present] grace and favor and [future] glory (honor, splendor, and heavenly bliss)! No good thing will He withhold from those who walk uprightly. Psalm 84:11, AMP

Your word I have hidden in my heart, that I might not sin against You. Blessed are You, O Lord! Teach me Your statutes. With my lips I have declared all the judgments of Your mouth. I have rejoiced in the way of Your testimonies, as much as in all riches. I will meditate on Your precepts, and contemplate Your ways. I will delight myself in Your statutes; I will not forget Your word. Psalm 119:11-16, NKJV

The faithful love of the Lord never ends! His mercies never cease. Lamentations 3:22, NLT

Since, then, you have been raised with Christ, set your hearts on things above, where Christ is seated at the right hand of God. Set your minds on things above, not on earthly things. For you died, and your life is now hidden with Christ in God. When Christ, who is your life, appears, then you also will appear with him in glory. Colossians 3:1-4, NIV

Control Myth - Experiencing freedom from concern about what others think of you will happen as you allow God to bring peace, moment-by-moment, deep within your soul. Relying on Him, you can be 100% responsible for your own emotional state rather than allowing other people's choices to control you. You will also realize the futility of trying to "make" other people happy and will realize they, too, are 100% responsible for their own lives. You don't have to be dominated by the futility of trying to control your world.

For God is the King of all the earth; sing to him a psalm of praise. God reigns over the nations; God is seated on his holy throne. The nobles of the nations assemble as the people of the God of Abraham, for the kings of the earth belong to God; he is greatly exalted. Psalm 47:7-9, NIV

I will lift up my eyes to the hills – from whence comes my help? My help comes from the Lord, Who made heaven and earth. He will not allow your foot to be moved; He who keeps you will not slumber. Behold, He who keeps Israel shall neither slumber nor sleep. Psalm 121:1-4, NKJV

And now, just as you accepted Christ Jesus as your Lord, you must continue to follow him. Let your roots grow down into him, and let your lives be built on him. Then your faith will grow strong in the truth you were taught, and you will overflow with thankfulness.

Don't let anyone capture you with empty philosophies and high-sounding nonsense that come from human thinking and from the spiritual powers of this world, rather than from Christ. For in Christ lives all the fullness of God in a human body. So you also are complete through your union with Christ, who is the head over every ruler and authority. Colossians 2:6-10, NLT

I am the Alpha and the Omega, the Beginning and the End, says the Lord God, He Who is and Who was and Who is to come, the Almighty (the Ruler of all). Revelation 1:8, AMP

Overlooking the Positive - God's Word brings lasting hope, unfailing love, and clear affirmation that can help you in every area of life. You can be confident in His Presence.

And we know that God causes everything to work together for the good of those who love God and are called according to his purpose for them.

What shall we say about such wonderful things as these? If God is for us, who can ever be against us? Since he did not spare even his own Son but gave him up for us all, won't he also give us everything else? Who dares accuse us whom God has chosen for his own? No one—for God himself has given us right standing with himself. Who then will condemn us? No one—for Christ Jesus died for us and was raised to life for us, and he is sitting in the place of honor at God's right hand, pleading for us.

Can anything ever separate us from Christ's love? Does it mean he no longer loves us if we have trouble or calamity, or are persecuted, or hungry, or destitute, or in danger, or threatened with death? (As the Scriptures say, "For your sake we are killed every day; we are being slaughtered like sheep.") No, despite all these things, overwhelming victory is ours through Christ, who loved us.

And I am convinced that nothing can ever separate us from God's love. Neither death nor life, neither angels nor demons, neither our fears for today nor our worries about tomorrow—not even the powers of hell can separate us from God's love. No power in the sky above or in the earth below—indeed, nothing in all creation will ever be able to separate us from the love of God that is revealed in Christ Jesus our Lord. Romans 8:28; 31-39, NLT

God's divine power has given us everything we need for life and for godliness. This power was given to us through knowledge of the one who called us by his own glory and integrity. Through his glory and integrity he has given us his promises that are of the highest value. Through these promises you will share in the divine nature because you have escaped the corruption that sinful desires cause in the world.

Because of this, make every effort to add integrity to your faith; and to integrity add knowledge; to knowledge add self-control; to self-control add endurance; to endurance add godliness; to godliness add Christian affection; and to Christian affection add love. If you have these qualities and they are increasing, it demonstrates that your knowledge about our Lord Jesus Christ is living and productive. If these qualities aren't present in your life, you're shortsighted and have forgotten that you were cleansed from your past sins. Therefore, brothers and sisters, use more effort to make God's calling and choosing of you secure. 2 Peter 1:3-10, GW

Journaling to Freedom & Joy

Use the following three-step process as you journal.

1. Write down your automatic negative thought(s).
2. Identify the type(s) of cognitive distortions (see pages 29-30).
3. Write a different thought from what you have been thinking (something that does not result in your feeling depressed, anxious, etc.). See Appendix A for ideas, because step three is the most important part of this process.

1. Automatic negative thought(s).

2. Type(s) of cognitive distortion.

3. New Healing Thought(s). A healing, positive thought (something that does not result in your feeling depressed, anxious, etc.). See Appendix A for Scripture verses to replace negative automatic thoughts and restore your soul.

The Chaff Chart

The *CHAFF* Chart helps you understand that *Circumstances, Health, Appearance, Family or Friends* and/or *Finances* can all be chaff. Though each element in the chart is a useful part of life; it is not worthy of being life's purpose. The chart provides a place to write down the times you rely on any form of CHAFF instead of on God. Through God's grace and power, you can learn to live in His provision instead of the world's temporary satisfaction. Ask God to search your heart, thanking Him that He can use CHAFF as a vehicle of growth in your life, then write down recent times you have depended on CHAFF rather than God for peace, hope, purpose, joy, or comfort.

Circumstances	
Health	
Appearance	
Family or Friends	
Finances	

Observe - Interpret - Apply

One of the best ways to make Scripture come alive is to discover God's leading and direction through the study of His Word. Select the passage you want to study. Read it carefully and prayerfully several times. As you read, **observe** the facts. Write names, key words, questions, etc., anything that piques your curiosity. Begin to **interpret** by gaining understanding and finding answers to your questions. A good study Bible is very helpful as well as online sources such as www.biblegateway.com. Once you are satisfied you know the meaning of the passage, **apply** it to your life and the circumstances you are currently facing. Remember, you are reading God's love letter to you!

Observe What do I see?	Interpret What does it mean?	Apply How can I apply it to my life?
Passage to be studied:		

Promises to claim:

Date studied: _____

Sins to confess:

Grounding Exercises

Grounding exercises are helpful whenever you feel overwhelmed by traumatic memories, sadness, feelings of anxiety, anger or inexplicable fears. These challenging emotions can be activated by any of your five senses—such as seeing or smelling something that reminds you of past trauma. It only takes a fraction of a second for traumatic memories stored in the brain's emotional regulator, the amygdala, to "hijack" the brain's CEO, the prefrontal cortex (PFC). When a "hijacking" occurs, be alert for any indication of the *Five Fs* (Fight, Flight, Freeze, Fornicate, or Feed). The presence of one or more "F" indicators is a reminder for you to immediately ground yourself. You can consciously move your thoughts back into your brain's prefrontal cortex as rapidly as they left there (see 2 Corinthians 10:5).

Applying positive self-talk to move out of a "hijacking," you can choose from any of the following grounding exercises to help you live in the here-and-now instead of in past trauma.

1. **Physical Grounding**: if seated, press your hands into the chair/sofa where you're seated and simply notice fabrics, textures, etc.; or stand and observe the sensations of your feet touching the floor. Then, press the palms of your hands together and be aware of the sensation of stretching. Or, try a 4-D exercise—stand up, and take time to fully stretch your body north, south, west, and then east. Another option is to go outside and take a walk, observing where you are, using all five of your senses.

2. **Mental Grounding**: describe shapes or colors in the room or place where you are; count backwards from 100 by 5's; solve a basic math problem; write down a list of things you like to do; recall favorite places you've visited; name sports teams, dog breeds, types of flowers, birds, etc. Or, imagine a large container with a tightly-fitting lid; quickly open the container and put the distressing thoughts into it, sealing them with the lid, then mentally place that sealed container far away from you. Review the sample positive self-talk statements on this and the following page.

3. **Soothing Grounding**: Instead of allowing intrusive traumatic memories to govern your life or shift your focus to painful feelings, you can think calmly, breathing deeply. You can consciously choose to talk to yourself with kindness and dignity, thinking with a gentle internal voice. You can remind yourself that you have a future and a hope. You can review the Scripture verses on this and the following page. Focus on God's promises. For example, the *Lord is gracious, merciful, and full of loving compassion* (Psalm 111:4, Amplified).

Practicing Positive Self-Talk

Often survivors of sexual abuse talk to themselves in a negative way—not at all like they would speak to anyone else. We can all learn to talk to ourselves in a kinder, gentler way than we sometimes do. Think of how you might calm a crying baby—speaking with a soft, soothing voice. Then imagine how you speak to yourself when you feel anxious or sad. Are you harsh or negative when you talk to yourself? The statements on this and the following page can help you develop positive self-talk.

When you feel symptoms of anxiety, fear or worry, how you talk to yourself determines how rapidly you will move beyond difficult emotions or even initial physiological symptoms* of a panic attack [*symptoms such as chest pain and shortness of breath should be evaluated by a medical doctor]. Your proactive mental choices can shorten debilitating symptoms to minutes instead of hours.

Any of the following sample statements and Scripture verses can help you build a positive self-talk "vocabulary." You can put any of these statements and verses on your phone, laptop or index cards, to use as needed. **You can choose what you think!**

❖ This feeling is uncomfortable, but I can acknowledge it, face it and move beyond it, trusting in God. He says: *Do not fear, for I am with you; do not anxiously look about you, for I am your God. I will strengthen you, surely I will help you, surely I will uphold you with My righteous right hand* (Isaiah 41:10, NASU).

The Lord is my light and my salvation – whom shall I fear? The Lord is the stronghold of my life – of whom shall I be afraid? (Psalm 27:1, NIV)

❖ I can trust God during this difficult time, even if no one else seems to notice or care.

I call to God; God will help me. At dusk, dawn, and noon I sigh deep sighs – he hears, he rescues. My life is well and whole, secure in the middle of danger even while thousands are lined up against me. God hears it all, and from his judge's bench puts them in their place. But, set in their ways, they won't change; they pay him no mind. And this, my best friend, betrayed his best friends; his life betrayed his word. All my life I've been charmed by his speech, never dreaming he'd turn on me. His words, which were music to my ears, turned to daggers in my heart.

Pile your troubles on God's shoulders – he'll carry your load, he'll help you out. He'll never let good people topple into ruin. But you, God, will throw the others into a muddy bog, cut the lifespan of assassins and traitors in half.

And I trust in you. (Psalm 55:16-22, The Message)

❖ I will ask God to show me my root issues or fears and allow Him to heal me from the inside out.

Search me, O God, and know my heart; try me and know my anxious thoughts; and see if there be any hurtful way in me, and lead me in the everlasting way. (Psalm 139:23-24, NASU)

❖ This will pass.

I sought the Lord, and He answered me, and delivered me from all my fears. (Psalm 34:4, NASU)

❖ This is just anxiety; I'm not going to let it define me.

In the multitude of my [anxious] thoughts within me, Your comforts cheer and delight my soul! (Psalm 94:19, Amplified)

❖ I will choose to focus on solutions, not on problems, people, or things I cannot change.

Casting the whole of your care [all your anxieties, all your worries, all your concerns, once and for all] on Him, for He cares for you affectionately and cares about you watchfully. [Psalm 55:22.] (1 Peter 5:7, Amplified)

❖ I can survive—and thrive!

May the Master take you by the hand and lead you along the path of God's love and Christ's endurance. (2 Thessalonians 3:5, The Message)

Works Cited

Chapter One

1. Bromley, Nicole Braddock. *Hush: Moving from Silence to Healing after Childhood Sexual Abuse*. Page 28. Moody Press, 2007. Print.
2. Knauer, Sandra, LCSW. *Recovering from Sexual Abuse, Addictions, and Compulsive Behaviors "Numb" Survivors*. Page 65. The Haworth Press, Inc., 2002. Print.
3. Allender, Dan B. *The Wounded Heart*. Page 91. NavPress, 1990. Print.
4. Allender, Dan B. *The Wounded Heart*. Page 157. NavPress, 1990. Print.
5. Bromley, Nicole Braddock. *Hush: Moving from Silence to Healing after Childhood Sexual Abuse*. Page 129. Moody Press, 2007. Print.
6. Young, Sarah. *Jesus Calling: A 365-Day Journaling Devotion – October 23*. Thomas Nelson, 2008. Print.
7. Bromley, Nicole Braddock. *Hush: Moving from Silence to Healing after Childhood Sexual Abuse*. Page 72. Moody Press, 2007. Print.
8. Newman, Barbara M., and Philip R. Newman. *Development Through Life: A Psychosocial Approach*. 8th ed. Pages 60-61. Wadsworth/Thompson, 2003. Print.
9. Stoop, Dr. David and Masteller, Dr. James. *Forgiving our Parents Forgiving Ourselves: Healing Adult Children of Dysfunctional Families*. Page 289-290. Regal Books, 1991. Print.
10. Young, Sarah. *Jesus Calling: A 365-Day Journaling Devotion - September 30*. Thomas Nelson, 2008. Print.

Chapter Two

11. Donehey, Mike / Ingram, Jason / LaRue, Phillip. "Tenth Avenue North." Lyrics. 2010. Provident Label Group LLC. 11 September 2010. <http://www.tenthavenuenorth.com/music>.
12. Nouwen, Henry J. M. "Henry J.M. Nouwen." The Return of the Prodigal Son. 2003. 13 September 2010. <http://www.atma-o-jibon.org/english/nouwen_return5.htm>.
13. Lloyd-Jones, Martyn. "Martyn Lloyd-Jones Quotes, Page 3." oChristian Quotes. 1999-2010. oChristian.com. 15 September 2010. <http://christian-quotes.ochristian.com/Martyn-Lloyd-Jones-Quotes/page-3.shtml>.
14. Mason, Mike. *The Gospel According to Job: An Honest Look at Pain from the Life of One Who Lost Everything*. Page 418. Crossway Books, 1994. Print.
15. Briscoe, Jill. "Beliefnet." Quote Library. Beliefnet Inc. 15 September 2010. <http://www.beliefnet.com/Quotes/Christian/J/Jill-Briscoe/I-Discovered-That-Sorrow-Was-Not-To-Be-Feared-But.aspx>.
16. Chambers, Oswald. *My Utmost for His Highest*. Page 215. Dodd, Mead & Company, 1935. Print.
17. Peterson, John W. "Home with God." Shepherd of Love. HomewithGod Christian Resources. 17 September 2010. <http://my.homewithgod.com/heavenlymidis2/shepherd.html>.
18. Swindoll, Charles R. "Thinkexist.com." Charles R. Swindoll Quotes. 1999-2010. ThinkExist.com Quotations. 10 October 2010. <http://thinkexist.com/quotation/the_longer_i_live-the_more_i_realize_the_impact/296740.html>.
19. Altman, Louise & George. "The Intentional Workplace." The Four Rooms of Wellness – How to Live in Them. 30 April 2010. The Intentional Workplace. 18 January 2011. <http://intentionalworkplace.com/2010/04/30/your-four-rooms-of-wellness-how-to-live-in-them/>.
20. Unknown. "MindTools." Personal Goal Setting. 1995-2010. Mind Tools, Ltd. 12 October 2010. <http://www.mindtools.com/page6.html>.
21. Newman, Barbara M., and Philip R. Newman. *Development Through Life: A Psychosocial Approach*. 8th ed. Pages 60-61. Wadsworth/Thompson, 2003. Print.
22. Postman, Neil. "Quotations About Children." The Quote Garden. 1998-2011. 17 January 2011. <http://www.quotegarden.com/children.html>.
23. Young, Sarah. *Jesus Calling: A 365-Day Journaling Devotion - September 24*. Thomas Nelson, 2008. Print.

Chapter Three

24. Einstein, Albert. "The Quote Garden." Quotations About L. 1998-2010. Terri Guillemets (1973-) U.S. quotation anthologistcreator of The Quote Garden. 29 November 2010. <http://www.quotegarden.com/thinking.html>.
25. Holmes, Oliver Wendell. "The Quote Garden." Quotations About Language. 1998-2010. Terri Guillemets (1973-) U.S. quotation anthologistcreator of The Quote Garden. 29 November 2010. <http://www.quotegarden.com/language.html>.
26. Young, Sarah. *Jesus Calling: A 365-Day Journaling Devotion – May 9*. Thomas Nelson, 2008. Print.
27. Chesterson, G.K. "All Great Quotes." Fairy Tale Quotes. 2010. Famous Quotes. 29 November 2010. <http://www.allgreatquotes.com/fairy_tale_quotes.shtml>.
28. Southey, Robert. "Thinkexist.com." Robert Southey Quotes. 1999-2010. ThinkExist.com Quotations. 1 December 2010. < http://thinkexist.com/quotes/robert_southey/>.
29. Mason, Mike. *Champagne for the Soul: An Experiment in Joy*. Page 130. Waterbrook, 2003. Print.
30. Newman, Barbara M., and Philip R. Newman. *Development Through Life: A Psychosocial Approach*. 8th ed. Pages 60-61. Wadsworth/Thompson, 2003. Print.
31. Keller, Helen. "Purpose Quotes." Inspirational Words of Wisdom. Undefined. 16 December 2010. <http://www.wow4u.com/purpose-photo/index.html>.

Chapter Four

32. Hall, John Mark. "Casting Crowns Lyrics: Who Am I." Song Lyrics. 2000-2010. eLyrics.net. 21 December 2010. http://www.elyrics.net/read/c/casting-crowns-lyrics/who-am-i-lyrics.html.
33. Young, Sarah. *Jesus Calling: A 365-Day Journaling Devotion – December 21*. Thomas Nelson, 2008. Print.
34. Author Unknown. "Quotations About God." The Quote Garden. 1998-2011. 24 January 2011. <http://www.quotegarden.com/god.html>.
35. Newman, Barbara M., and Philip R. Newman. *Development Through Life: A Psychosocial Approach*. 8th ed. Pages 60-61. Wadsworth/Thompson, 2003. Print.
36. Mason, Mike. *Champagne for the Soul: An Experiment in Joy*. Page 8. Waterbrook, 2003. Print.

Chapter Five

37. Ten Boom, Corrie. "goodreads." Corrie Ten Boom Quotes. 2011. Goodreads, Inc. 17 March 2011. <http://www.goodreads.com/author/quotes/102203.Corrie_Ten_Boom>.
38. Moore, Beth. *A Quick Word with Beth Moore: Quotations from When Godly People Do Ungodly Things – The Past*. B&H Publishing Group, 2009. Print.
39. Moore, Beth. *A Quick Word with Beth Moore: Quotations from When Godly People Do Ungodly Things – Cleansing*. B&H Publishing Group, 2009. Print.
40. Fuller, Thomas. "*Thomas Fuller Quotes*." Brainy Quote. 2011. BrainyMedia.com. 17 March 2011. < http://www.brainyquote.com/quotes/quotes/t/thomasfull378779.html>.
41. Mac, Toby. "*Toby Mac Lyrics*." *Suddenly*. 2000-2011. AZLyrics.com. 19 March 2011. <http://www.azlyrics.com/lyrics/tobymac/suddenly.html>.
42. Young, Sarah. *Jesus Calling: A 365-Day Journaling Devotion – October 16*. Thomas Nelson, 2008. Print.
43. Beattie, Melody. "*A Little Honesty Goes a Long Ways*." *Living in the Mystery*. 2011. Melody Beattie. 19 Mar 2011. <http://melodybeattie.com/blog/>.
44. Newman, Barbara M., and Philip R. Newman. *Development Through Life: A Psychosocial Approach*. 8th ed. Pages 60-61. Wadsworth/Thompson, 2003. Print.
45. "Freedom from Want." *Reader's Digest* Mar. 2011: 105-09. Print.
46. Luther, Martin. *Hymns for the Family of God*. A Mighty Fortress is Our God. Page 118. Paragon Associates, Inc. 1976. Print.

Chapter Six

47. Nouwen, Henri. "Henri Nouwen on Forgiveness." SamMarsh.net. 24 December 2008. SamMarsh.net. 13 April 2011. <http://www.sammarsh.net/?p=246>.
48. Wiesel, Elie. *Night*. Page xv. Hill and Wang, 2006. Print.

49. Yancey, Philip. "Forgiveness: It Just Ain't Fair." 30 Good Minutes. Chicago Sunday Evening Club. 13 April 2011. <http://www.csec.org/csec/sermon/yancey_3622.htm>.

50. Ten Boom, Corrie. "Thinkexist.com." *Corrie Ten Boom Quotes.* 1999-2010. ThinkExist.com Quotations. 14 April 2011. < http://thinkexist.com/quotes/corrie_ten_boom/>.

51. Ziglar, Zig. *INSPIRATION 365 Days A Year.* March 13. Simple Truths, 2008. Print.

52. Tutu, Desmond. "Thinkexist.com." *Bishop Desmond Tutu Quotes.* 1999-2010. ThinkExist.com Quotations. 18 April 2011. http://thinkexist.com/quotation/if_you_are_neutral_in_situations_of_injustice-you/200264.html.

53. Tutu, Desmond. "goodreads." *Desmond Tutu quotes.* Goodreads. 2010. 3 September 2010. <http://www.goodreads.com/quotes/show/81497

54. Smedes, Lewis B. *The Art of Forgiving: When You Need to Forgive and Don't Know How.* Page 176. Ballantine Books, 1996. Print.

55. Young, Sarah. *Jesus Calling: A 365-Day Journaling Devotion – June 2.* Thomas Nelson, 2008. Print.

Chapter Seven

56. Smedes, Lewis B. *The Art of Forgiving: When You Need to Forgive and Don't Know How.* Pages 35-36. Ballantine Books, 1996. Print.

57. Smedes, Lewis B. *The Art of Forgiving: When You Need to Forgive and Don't Know How.* Page 162. Ballantine Books, 1996. Print.

58. Brauns, Chris. *Unpacking Forgiveness: Biblical Answers for Complex Questions and Deep Wounds.* Page 165. Crossway Books, 2008. Print.

59. Walton, William H. "Quotations About Anger." The Quote Garden. 1998-2011. 20 April 2011. <http://www.quotegarden.com/anger.html>.

60. Stoop, Dr. David and Masteller, Dr. James. *Forgiving our Parents Forgiving Ourselves: Healing Adult Children of Dysfunctional Families.* Page 219. Regal Books, 1991. Print.

61. Smedes, Lewis B. *The Art of Forgiving: When You Need to Forgive and Don't Know How.* Page 62-63. Ballantine Books, 1996. Print.

62. King, Martin Luther, Jr. "Forgiveness is not an occasional act; it is a permanent attitude." Martin Luther King, Jr. – Resources for Dreamers. 10 November 2009. . 25 April 2011. <http://dream.phildavis.us/?p=31>.

63. Nouwen, Henri. "Quotes." The Forgiveness Foundation. 2005-2010. Forgiveness Foundation. 25 April 2011. <http://www.forgivenessfoundation.org/inspiration/quotes/>.

64. MacArthur, John. "Forgiveness Quotations." The Forgiveness Web. 12 December 2010. Heather P. Wilson, Ph.D. 28 April 2011.

65. Smedes, Lewis B. "Keys to Forgiving." *Christianity Today* 45.15 (2001): 73. Print.

66. Osiek, Carolyn. "Forgiveness Quotes." A Space Within. 2009. 29 April 2011. <http://www.aspacewithin.com/forgiveness-quotes.html>.

67. Wiesel, Elie. *Night.* Page 118. Hill and Wang, 2006. Print.

68. Leman, Dr. Kevin. *Have a New You by Friday.* Page 118. Revell, 2010. Print.

Chapter Eight

69. Lewis, C. S. *Mere Christianity.* Page 190. Macmillan Publishing Company, 1952. Print.

70. Lewis, C. S. *Mere Christianity.* Pages 53-54. Macmillan Publishing Company, 1952. Print.

71. Moore, Beth. *A Quick Word with Beth Moore: Quotations from When Godly People Do Ungodly Things – Condemnation.* B&H Publishing Group, 2009. Print.

72. Munroe, Myles. *In Pursuit of Purpose.* Page 14. Destiny Image Publishers, 1992. Print.

73. Young, Sarah. *Jesus Calling: A 365-Day Journaling Devotion – November 14.* Thomas Nelson, 2008. Print.

74. Leman, Dr. Kevin. *Have a New You by Friday.* Page 84. Revell, 2010. Print.

75. Anderson, Mac, compiler. *Motivational Quotes.* Page 32. Simple Truths, 2008. Print.

76. Stoop, Dr. David and Masteller, Dr. James. *Forgiving our Parents Forgiving Ourselves: Healing Adult Children of Dysfunctional Families.* Page 170. Regal Books, 1991. Print.

77. Benner, David G. *The Gift of Being Yourself: The Sacred Call to Self-Discovery.* Page 58. InterVarsity Press, 2004. Print.

78. Anderson, Mac, compiler. *Motivational Quotes*. Page 54. Simple Truths, 2008. Print.

79. Spurgeon, C.H. "Morning and Evening: Daily Meditations - May 18 AM." Christian Classics Ethereal Library. CCEL. 18 May 2011. <http://www.ccel.org/ccel/spurgeon/morneve.d0518am.html>.

80. Tada, Joni Eareckson. *When God Weeps: Why Our Sufferings Matter to the Almighty*. Page 166. Zondervan Publishing House, 1997. Print.

81. *Diagnostic and Statistical Manual of Mental Disorders*. Fourth Edition, Text Revision. Pages 386-389. American Psychiatric Association, 2000. Print.

82. Selye, Hans M.D. *The Stress of Life*. Pages 261-262. McGraw-Hill Book Company, 1956. Print.

83. Benner, David G. *The Gift of Being Yourself: The Sacred Call to Self-Discovery*. Page 91. InterVarsity Press, 2004. Print.

84. Bromley, Nicole Braddock. *Hush: Moving from Silence to Healing after Childhood Sexual Abuse*. Page 173. Moody Press, 2007. Print.

85. Newman, Barbara M., and Philip R. Newman. *Development Through Life: A Psychosocial Approach*. 8th ed. Pages 60-61. Wadsworth/Thompson, 2003. Print.

86. Schwartz, Mel, L.C.S.W. "A Shift of Mind." Who Am I? 2 June 2010. Psychology Today. 11 May 2011. <http://www.psychologytoday.com/blog/shift-mind/201006/who-am-i>.

Chapter Nine

87. Warren, Rick. *The Purpose Driven Life*. Page 17. Zondervan, 2002. Print.

88. Munroe, Myles. *In Pursuit of Purpose*. Page 8. Destiny Image Publishers, 1992. Print.

89. Miller, Arthur F. and Mattson, Ralph T. *The TRUTH about you: Discover what you should be doing with your life*. Page 15. Revell, 1977. Print.

90. Warren, Rick. *The Purpose Driven Life*. Page 55. Zondervan, 2002. Print.

91. Frankl, Viktor E. *Man's Search for Meaning*. Page 91. Washington Square Press, 1984. Print.

92. Mother Teresa. "Mother Teresa quotes." Search Quotes. 2011. SearchQuotes.com. 06 June 2011. <http://www.searchquotes.com/quotation/In_this_life_we_cannot_do_great_things._We_can_only_do_small_things_with_great_love/20658/>.

93. Frankl, Viktor E. *Man's Search for Meaning*. Page 133. Washington Square Press, 1984. Print.

94. Tripp, Paul David. *Instruments in the Redeemer's Hands*. Page 154. P&R Publishing, 2002. Print.

95. Munroe, Myles. *In Pursuit of Purpose*. Page 14. Destiny Image Publishers, 1992. Print.

96. Frankl, Viktor E. "Viktor E. Frankl Quotes." Brainy Quote. 2011. BrainyMedia.com. 07 June 2011. <http://www.brainyquote.com/quotes/quotes/v/viktorefr126225.html>.

97. Acappella. "Acappella Lyrics." Lyrics.Time. 2011. Lyricstime.com. 07 June 2011. <http://www.lyricstime.com/acappella-more-than-conquerors-lyrics.html>.

98. Chambers, Oswald. *Daily Thoughts for Disciples*. Page 47. Zondervan, 1976. Print.

99. Bryne, Mary E., translator. "Be Thou My Vision." Great Christian Hymns. 2005-2009. GreatChristianHymns.com. 08 June 2011. <http://www.greatchristianhymns.com/be-thou-my-vision.html>.

100. Bryne, Mary E., translator. "Be Thou My Vision." Great Christian Hymns. 2005-2009. GreatChristianHymns.com. 08 June 2011. <http://www.greatchristianhymns.com/be-thou-my-vision.html>.

101. Newman, Barbara M., and Philip R. Newman. *Development Through Life: A Psychosocial Approach*. 8th ed. Pages 60-61. Wadsworth/Thompson, 2003. Print.

Chapter Ten

102. Metaxas, Eric. *Amazing Grace*. Page 215. Harper San Francisco, 2007. Print.

103. Yancey, Philip. *Soul Survivor*. Page 1. Doubleday, 2001. Print.

104. Yancey, Philip. *Soul Survivor*. Page 45. Doubleday, 2001. Print.

105. Nouwen, Henri. "Quotes about Spiritual Abuse." angles. 22 February 2010. Disciple of Christ. 08 June 2011. <https://benjaminchew110478.wordpress.com/tag/quotes-about-spiritual-abuse/>.

106. Mason, Mike. *Practicing the Presence of People*. Page 45. Waterbrook Press, 1999. Print.

107. Smalley, Gary and Trent, John, Ph.D. *The Blessing*. Page 19. Thomas Nelson Publishers, 1986. Print.

108. Clairmont, Patsy. "goodreads." Patsy Clairmont Quotes. 2011. Goodreads, Inc. 16 June 2011. <http://www.goodreads.com/quotes/show/204259>.

109. Briscoe, Jill. *Renewal on the Run.* Page 48. New Hope Publishers, 2005. Print.

110. Wulf, Dick. *Find Yourself, Give Yourself.* Pages 20-21. NavPress, 1983. Print.

111. McGrath, Joanna and McGrath, Alister. *Self-Esteem: The Cross and Christian Confidence.* Page 143. Crossway Books, 2002. Print.

112. Allender, Dr. Dan B. and Longman III, Dr. Tremper. *Bold Love.* Page 89. NavPress, 1992. Print.

113. Wulf, Dick. *Find Yourself, Give Yourself.* Page158. NavPress, 1983. Print.

114. Tripp, Paul David. *Instruments in the Redeemer's Hands.* Page 193. P&R Publishing, 2002. Print.

115. Theroux, Alexander. "Belonging Quotes." Brainy Quote. 2011. BrainyMedia.com. 10 June 2011. <http://www.brainyquote.com/quotes/keywords/belonging.html>.

116. Mason, Mike. *Practicing the Presence of People.* Page 69-70. Waterbrook Press, 1999. Print.

117. Swindoll, Luci. "Genuine In Christ." The Master's Touch. Undefined. FollowYourDreams.net. 12 June 2011. <http://www.followyourdreams.net/TheMastersTouch/genuine.html>.

118. Ziglar, Zig. *INSPIRATION 365 Days A Year.* June 16. Simple Truths, 2008. Print.

119. Carver, George Washington. "Quotation Details." The Quotations Page. 1994-2010. Michael Moncur. 11 June 2011. <http://www.quotationspage.com/quote/26308.html>.

120. Casting Crowns. "If We Are The Body Lyrics." sing365.com. 2000-2011. sing365.com. 11 June 2011. <http://www.sing365.com/music/lyric.nsf/if-we-are-the-body-lyrics-casting-crowns/617d1b30e33f493848256e9c000db757>.

121. Chesterton, Gilbert K. "Gilbert K. Chesterton Quotes." Brainy Quote. 2011. BrainyMedia.com. 11 June 2011. <http://www.brainyquote.com/quotes/quotes/g/gilbertkc140975.html>.

122. Newman, Barbara M., and Philip R. Newman. *Development Through Life: A Psychosocial Approach.* 8th ed. Pages 60-61. Wadsworth/Thompson, 2003. Print.

123. Ecker, Richard E. *The Stress Myth.* Page 34. Inter-Varsity Press, 1985. Print.

124. Young, Sarah. *Jesus Calling: A 365-Day Journaling Devotion – August 4.* Thomas Nelson, 2008. Print.

Chapter Eleven

125. Emerson, Ralph Waldo. "Ralph Waldo Emerson Quotes." Quote Cosmos. 2010. quotecosmos.com. 13 June 2011. <http://www.quotecosmos.com/quotes/10741/view>.

126. Emerald, David. *The Power of TED* (*the empowerment dynamic).* Page 16-17; 128. Polaris Publishing, 2006. Print.

127. Emerald, David. *The Power of TED* (*the empowerment dynamic).* Page 127. Polaris Publishing, 2006. Print.

128. Peeples, Dr. Sam, Jr. *A Stress Management Seminar.* Page 1. Christian Ministries, Inc. Print.

129. Emerald, David. *The Power of TED* (*the empowerment dynamic).* Page 119. Polaris Publishing, 2006. Print.

130. Newman, Barbara M., and Philip R. Newman. *Development Through Life: A Psychosocial Approach.* 8th ed. Pages 60-61. Wadsworth/Thompson, 2003. Print.

131. Edison, Thomas. "Authors." Quote DB. undefined. QuoteDB.com. 15 June 2011. <http://www.quotedb.com/quotes/1379>.

132. Ricker, Cheryl. *A Friend in the Storm.* Page 86. Zondervan, 2010. Print.

133. McFadden, Dr. Joseph "Tip". "2004 SPRING COMMENCEMENT TRANSCRIPT: DR. JOSEPH "TIP" MCFADDEN." UNK News. 10 May 2004. University of Nebraska Kearney. 15 June 2011. <http://www.unknews.com/UNK/story/?a=1518>.

134. McFadden, Dr. Joseph "Tip". "2004 SPRING COMMENCEMENT TRANSCRIPT: DR. JOSEPH "TIP" MCFADDEN." UNK News. 10 May 2004. University of Nebraska Kearney. 15 June 2011. <http://www.unknews.com/UNK/story/?a=1518>.

Chapter Twelve

135. Anderson, Mac, compiler. *Motivational Quotes.* Page 74. Simple Truths, 2008. Print.

136. Hendricks, Howard G. and Hendricks, William D. *Living by the Book.* Pages 64-65. Moody Press, 1991. Print.

137. Lloyd-Jones, D. Martyn. *Spiritual Depression: Its Causes and Its Cure.* Page 256. Wm. B. Eerdmans Publishing Company, 1965. Print.

138. Chambers, Oswald. *Oswald Chambers: The Best from All His Books.* Page 176. Oliver-Nelson Books, 1987. Print.

139. Lloyd-Jones, D. Martyn. *Spiritual Depression: Its Causes and Its Cure.* Page 101. Wm. B. Eerdmans Publishing Company, 1965. Print.

140. Spurgeon, Charles H. "Spurgeon's Daily Meditations - September 23, Morning." Spurgeon's Daily Devotionals. 23 September 2006. Free Republic, LLC. 16 June 2011. <http://www.freerepublic.com/focus/f-religion/1706818/posts>.

141. Moore, Beth. *A Quick Word with Beth Moore: Quotations from When Godly People Do Ungodly Things – Gratitude.* B&H Publishing Group, 2009. Print.

142. Lloyd-Jones, D. Martyn. *Spiritual Depression: Its Causes and Its Cure.* Page 110-111. Wm. B. Eerdmans Publishing Company, 1965. Print.

143. Munroe, Myles. *In Pursuit of Purpose.* Page 45. Destiny Image Publishers, 1992. Print.

144. Spurgeon, Charles H. "Morning - June 17." HEARTLIGHT. 1996-2011. HEARTLIGHT Magazine. 17 June 2011. <http://www.heartlight.org/spurgeon/0617-am.html>.

145. Crabb, Larry. *Shattered Dreams.* Back Cover. Waterbrook Press, 2001. Print.

146. Crabb, Larry. *Shattered Dreams.* Page 146. Waterbrook Press, 2001. Print.

147. Newman, Barbara M., and Philip R. Newman. *Development Through Life: A Psychosocial Approach.* 8th ed. Pages 60-61. Wadsworth/Thompson, 2003. Print.